LanguageCert Communicator
CEFR Level B2
ESOL/SELT 朗思全真模拟题 1

（英）安德鲁·贝蒂斯（Andrew Betsis） 编著
（英）劳伦斯·马马斯（Lawrence Mamas）

华中科技大学出版社
http://press.hust.edu.cn
中国·武汉

图书在版编目（CIP）数据

朗思全真模拟题 . 1 = LanguageCert Communicator CEFR Level B2 ESOL/SELT：英文 /（英）安德鲁·贝蒂斯,（英）劳伦斯·马马斯编著 . — 武汉：华中科技大学出版社，2022.12
ISBN 978-7-5680-8886-2

Ⅰ . ①朗… Ⅱ . ①安… ②劳… Ⅲ . ①英语水平考试—习题集 Ⅳ . ① H310.41-44

中国版本图书馆 CIP 数据核字 (2022) 第 238251 号

湖北省版权局著作权合同登记 图字：17-2022-143 号

朗思全真模拟题 1 LanguageCert Communicator CEFR Level B2 ESOL/SELT　　（英）安德鲁·贝蒂斯 编著
　　　　　　　　　　　　　　　　　　　　　　　　　　　　　　　　　　　　（英）劳伦斯·马马斯

策划编辑：熊元勇　阮　钏　傅　文　李娟娟
责任编辑：傅　文　马红静
封面设计：郎思哥
责任校对：刘小雨
责任监印：朱　玢
出版发行：华中科技大学出版社（中国·武汉）　　　　　　电话：（027）81321913
　　　　　武汉市东湖新技术开发区华工科技园　　　　　　邮编：430223
录　　排：华中科技大学惠友文印中心
印　　刷：武汉市籍缘印刷厂
开　　本：787 mm×1092 mm　1/16
印　　张：12.25
字　　数：224 千字
版　　次：2022 年 12 月第 1 版第 1 次印刷
定　　价：88.00 元

本书若有印装质量问题，请向出版社营销中心调换
全国免费服务热线：400-6679-118　竭诚为您服务
版权所有　侵权必究

Contents

No. 1
Practice Paper Tests

Practice Paper Test 1 002

Practice Paper Test 2 023

Practice Paper Test 3 045

Practice Paper Test 4 067

Practice Paper Test 5 089

No. 2
Speaking Tests ESOL

Test 1 112

Test 2 119

Test 3 127

Test 4 135

Test 5 143

No. 3
Audio Scripts

Test 1 152

Test 2 159

Test 3 166

Test 4 172

Test 5 179

About LanguageCert English Spoken Other Language (ESOL) Test 186

Answer Key 187

No.1

Practice Paper Tests

LanguageCert
Communicator B2
Level 1
International ESOL (Listening, Reading, Writing)
Practice Paper Test 1

Listening Test Audio

Candidate's name (block letters please)

Centre no   Date

Time allowed:

Listening   about 30 minutes

Reading and Writing   2 hours and 10 minutes

Instructions to Candidates

- An Answer Sheet will be provided.

- All answers must be transferred to the Answer Sheet.

- Please use a softpencil (2B, HB).

Listening Part 1

You will hear some short conversations. You will hear each conversation twice. Choose the correct answer for each conversation.

1. a) I can't today.
   b) In fifteen minutes.
   c) I didn't think so.

2. a) Oh no! I really want you to be there.
   b) There won't be that many people there.
   c) I'm sure I will.

3. a) I've met some people.
   b) I'd love to meet him.
   c) I will!

4. a) It is a bit funny, actually.
   b) I'm not sure, but I think she might be.
   c) I agree; it would be the best thing by far.

5. a) Well, maybe next year.
   b) Neither have I.
   c) I'm not sure.

6. a) We haven't made any plans to.
   b) There are lots of concerts this summer.
   c) I might take singing lessons.

7. a) I wouldn't expect it.
   b) I always thought so.
   c) That's because it's Sunday.

Listening Part 2

You will hear some conversations. You will hear each conversation twice. Choose the correct answers for each conversation.

Conversation 1

1. Where do the two speakers know each other from?
   a) they travelled together
   b) Law school
   c) university

2. The man and the woman
   a) have always been in touch.
   b) are going to get married.
   c) haven't seen each other for a long time.

Conversation 2

3. The man is
   a) a designer.
   b) the woman's friend.
   c) a furniture salesman.

4. The woman
   a) wants a specific colour for her bathroom.
   b) is reluctant to buy any new furniture.
   c) isn't sure yet about the colour in her bedroom.

Conversation 3

5. The two speakers are
   a) good friends.
   b) salesperson and customer.
   c) interviewer and interviewee.

6. What kind of work does the woman want to do?
   a) interacting with customers
   b) being behind the scenes
   c) seeing that things run smoothly

Listening Part 3

You will hear someone talking. You will hear the person twice. Complete the information. Write short answers of one to five words.

Summer Camp

1. Monday's main activity:
   ....

2. Tuesday through Thursday's activities include:
   ....

3. When children are at the lake there must be:
   ....

4. Where to have a barbecue on Thursday evening:
   ....

5. Report if any children have special:
   ....

6. What to do on Friday:
   ....

7. Friday's special surprise:
   ....

No.1 Practice Paper Tests

Listening Part 4

You will hear a conversation. You will hear the conversation twice. Choose the correct answers.

1. What categories would the woman's interests fall under?
   a) culture and fashion
   b) sightseeing and history
   c) adventure and exercise

2. The man and woman are going to stay in New York City
   a) for three weeks.
   b) for one week.
   c) for two weeks.

3. How do the man and woman seem to be feeling about the trip?
   a) nervous
   b) depressed
   c) excited

4. How much will the man and woman spend on their hotel for the week?
   a) $1,500
   b) $200
   c) $1,300

5. The man and woman want to visit Long Island in order
   a) to be near the water.
   b) to visit a relative.
   c) to get out of the city.

6. What sight does the man **not** want to visit?
   a) the Ground Zero Museum
   b) the Metropolitan Museum of Art
   c) the New York Fashion Museum

Reading Part 1

Read the text and the questions. Choose the correct answer for each question.

THE GHOST SLUG

A new kind of animal has just been discovered under a flowerpot in Wales. It's been called the 'ghost slug', and it is unusual for several reasons. This slug is large, reaching 6 or 7 cm in size. It has no eyes, and is white in colour. It is active at night, and unlike the majority of slugs, it is a carnivore, feeding on earthworms using its blade-like teeth. The species was unknown to science before 2006.

The first ghost slug was discovered in 2006 in Glamorgan, Wales, and was formally described and named in 2008 by Ben Rowson at the National Museum of Wales, and Bill Symondson, an ecologist at Cardiff University. Because of the slug's white colour and nocturnal habits, and because it has been so rarely seen, it was given the species name ysbryda. The word '*ysbryd*' means ghost in the Welsh language. This in turn gave rise to the common name, 'ghost slug'. This appears to be the first case of an animal being given a name from the Welsh language.

Slug species like the ghost slug are more commonly found in Turkey and Georgia; however, the ghost slug is different from all of these. It is also the first slug of this kind to be found in Western Europe. Although the ghost slug is almost certainly not native to Wales, where the ghost slug came from and how it made its way into Britain is still unknown. Bill Symondson thinks that the slug probably originally lived deep inside caves because it is completely white and has no eyes. He thinks that it possibly came from a cave system in Eastern Europe, and may have arrived in Wales in the soil of a potted plant.

The first ghost slug was found in a lane in Caerphilly on October 29th, 2006. This single specimen was photographed and then released. A year later, another slug was found by a gardener near Cardiff, Wales, where it was brought to the attention of the National Museum of Wales. Additional ghost slugs have been found in Gorseinon, near Swansea, Wales.

The ghost slug is not harmful to humans, but because it is an introduced species, scientists are asking the public to tell them any time they see one of the slugs. Scientists want to make sure that the ghost slug does not spread and eat so many earthworms that the earthworm populations get smaller, because earthworms are important for the soil and the environment.

1. What is NOT unusual about the ghost slug?
    a) It eats meat.
    b) It has no eyes.
    c) It is not from Wales.

2. What is unique about the slug's name?
    a) It comes from the Welsh language.
    b) Its spelling is difficult.
    c) It means ghost.

3. How did the ghost slugs get to Wales?
    a) Eastern Europeans took them to Britain.
    b) They were always there.
    c) It is not verified.

4. After it was photographed, the first ghost slug
    a) was killed.
    b) was kept in the museum.
    c) was set free.

5. The ghost slug could be harmful to

   a) humans.

   b) earthworm populations.

   c) the environment.

6. Overall, the Welsh ghost slug could be described as

   a) a dangerous animal.

   b) a mysterious animal.

   c) an unbelievable animal.

Reading Part 2

Read the text. Use the sentences to complete the text. Choose the correct sentence for each gap. There is one extra sentence you will not need.

Mount Monadnock

The word "*monadnock*" comes from the language of a Native American tribe called *Abenaki*. The word was used to describe a mountain, although the exact kind of mountain is uncertain. The word was adopted by early settlers of southern New Hampshire and later by American geologists.

Mount Monadnock is the most prominent New England mountain. It is one of the most-climbed mountains in the world. **1** ☐ The mountain is the highest point in Cheshire County, New Hampshire. It stands 965 metres tall and is nearly 610 metres above the surrounding landscape. **2** ☐

The mountain is also well known in literature. The famous American writers and philosophers Ralph Waldo Emerson and Henry David Thoreau were both frequent visitors and wrote fondly about it. **3** ☐ A bog near the summit and a rocky lookout off one of the trails are both named after him. Emerson also made the mountain the subject of one of his famous poems. **4** ☐

In 1858, Moses Cudworth built a hotel called *The Half Way House* on the side of the mountain. There was a steep, winding road called the 'Toll Road' leading up to it. **5** ☐ Today Mount Monadnock is open for hiking, backpacking, picnicking and snowshoeing, and offers amazing views of rural southern New Hampshire. There is a campground on the southeast side of the mountain; however, camping is not allowed anywhere else. **6** ☐ Parking areas are open from 6am to 8pm, 7 days a week in the summer.

A. Thoreau spent a great deal of time writing about things he saw on the mountain.

B. This is the landscape of two New Hampshire towns: Jaffrey and Dublin.

C. The hotel was very successful, until 1954 when it burned down.

D. Many famous hikers have been to its summit.

E. It costs $3 to park at the bottom of the mountain.

F. There is also a lookout named after Emerson.

G. However, the southwestern slopes of the mountain drain into Fassett Brook.

Reading Part 3

Read the four texts. Which text gives you the answer to each question? Choose the correct text (A-D) for each question.

A.

We've been camping for many years and have found many recipes that we like. Most are very easy and even kids can make them.

Everyone congregates around the campfire in the evening to talk about what they've done that day and to plan their next day. The great thing about this is that the cook is right there with everyone, included in all the conversations.

Grilled Banana & Peanut Butter Sandwiches

  * **Peanut butter**   * **Bread**
  * **Butter**   * **Banana**

Spread the peanut butter and bananas on the bread and then grill over the fire- easy!

B.

The Gelert Twister 4 is a tent with an innovative design, exclusive to GELERT. It gives camping a whole new twist. It is light enough for use by backpackers, and the design allows this spacious tent to be pitched in a matter of minutes, with no trouble or confusion, even in the dark! No more worries about having to set up camp before the sun sets.

Now, we have teamed up with PJ Camping and are offering you the chance to win a Gelert Twister 4 Tent!

C.

How are you? I was wondering if you are still around next weekend, because Katie and I were thinking about camping Friday and Saturday night at a campground up north, and we thought you'd like to join us.

My family has a tent and all sorts of camping supplies so you'd just have to bring a sleeping bag, clothing and yourself ! It looks like the weather should be great so I think it would be perfect timing.

Write back or call me as soon as you get this!

D.

For years, Greenfield State Park has been a haven for hikers, bikers and swimmers. This July the park will open up 25 new camping spots. This is great news for out-of-towners and locals alike as the next and closest campground is over an hour away.

Jon and Susan Pierce, who have been running the park for the last 20 years are excited about the new campground. "We've been trying to get the state to approve funding for this campground for almost ten years and we finally got everything sorted out".

Which text

1. is an invitation? ☐
2. is trying to promote something? ☐
3. suggests making something? ☐

Which text provides the answers to the following questions?

4. How many camping spots will be in the park? ☐

5. What would someone need to bring on the camping trip? ☐

6. How fast can the tent be set up? ☐

7. How difficult is cooking while camping? ☐

Reading Part 4

Read the text and answer the questions. Use a maximum of five words for each question.

Penguins in Danger

Raising a baby takes a lot of work, especially when that baby is a king penguin. Now, it looks like climate change will make life even harder for these birds. A new study suggests that warmer waters could shrink their numbers.

Most king penguins live on the Crozet Archipelago, a group of islands in the Indian Ocean, about 1,000 miles north of Antarctica. After the penguin chicks are born in November (which is summer in the Southern Hemisphere), both parents spend 4 months collecting fish, some of which they regurgitate to feed their offspring.

When the fish move to deeper waters in March, the adults leave their chicks alone for months. They swim hundreds of miles south. There, near the Antarctic ice, they spend the winter eating squid, fish and other sea creatures, to replenish their own energy stores. In October, nearly a year after their chicks were born, the parents return to feed and finish raising them.

Scientists from the French National Centre for Scientific Research (CNRS) in Strasbourg, France, have been studying king penguins on the Crozet Archipelago for a decade. Starting in 1998, Yvon Le Maho and colleagues implanted electronic ID tags under the skin of hundreds of penguins.

These are the same types of tags you might put in your dog or cat, so you can track them if they get lost. The tags have allowed Le Maho's team to identify individual birds and keep track of details about them, such as how long they live, whether they return from their winter trips, and if their chicks manage to survive the winter. It is important for the scientists to do this because they need to know these things about the penguins, so if it seems they are in trouble, they can take steps to help them and ensure their survival.

To see whether water temperatures affect the penguins, Le Maho compared his data with temperature records. Ocean surface temperatures vary from year to year. And previous research had shown that fewer squid, fish and other creatures are present when the water is warmer. Le Maho suspected that this drop in the food supply would make it harder for adult penguins to survive the tough times ahead. Indeed, his results showed that fewer adults survived during winters when the water was especially warm. Just a quarter of a degree (0.26℃ to be exact) warming of seawater reduces adult penguins' survival rates by 9 percent in later years.

King penguins can live for up to 30 years. And for now, the population still appears healthy. But a warming trend could spell big trouble for a bird that depends on cold and ice.

1. Why are penguins born in November, and not in May?

   ....

2. What do king penguins do after their babies are born?

   ....

3. What do parent penguins do in March, when they leave their chicks?

   ....

4. In what month do parent penguins return to their young?

   ....

5. Where on the penguins did scientists put electronic ID tags?

   ....

6. What does sometimes cause the levels of penguins' food supplies to drop?

   ....

7. How old do king penguins live to be?

   ....

Writing Part 1

Write an **article** for an English language magazine, in response to the notice below, trying to persuade some of the subscribers of this magazine to visit the place you recommend.

 Be sure to describe
- where the place is located
- what there is to do there
- what makes that place special

Write between 100 and 150 words.

Vacation Destination

We are looking for articles about interesting places for holidays. Choose a place, close to your home or far away, to write about. We want to hear about a place that you have visited and think other readers would like to visit, too. The winner will have their article published in next month's magazine. Send entries to Jamie Fox, Vacation Destination, 21, Bond Street, Leicester, UK.

No.1 Practice Paper Tests

Writing Part 2

Write a **composition** for your English class describing someone who you respect and look up to. Explain why you feel the way you do about that person. What important qualities does this person have?

Write between 150 and 200 words.

No.1 Practice Paper Tests

LanguageCert
Communicator B2
Level 1
International ESOL (Listening, Reading, Writing)
Practice Paper Test 2

Listening Test Audio

Candidate's name (block letters please)

Centre no   **Date**

Time allowed:

Listening   about 30 minutes

Reading and Writing   2 hours and 10 minutes

Instructions to Candidates

- An Answer Sheet will be provided.

- All answers must be transferred to the Answer Sheet.

- Please use a softpencil (2B, HB).

Listening Part 1

You will hear some short conversations. You will hear each conversation twice. Choose the correct answer for each conversation.

1. a) In ten minutes.
   b) I'm going to the gym.
   c) I'm positive of it.

2. a) I wouldn't count on it.
   b) There aren't any paintings.
   c) Do you think so?

3. a) Oh! Not at all! Good idea!
   b) Of course I would!
   c) I'll repeat it then.

4. a) I'm cold now.
   b) Here I am.
   c) I agree.

5. a) There was sun, too.
   b) But that's when we're going camping!
   c) But don't you want to get out of the house?

6. a) I was thinking about it.
   b) We shouldn't.
   c) How come?

7. a) As long as she does, you can.
   b) I don't think so.
   c) There isn't room in the car.

Listening Part 2

You will hear some conversations. You will hear each conversation twice. Choose the correct answers for each conversation.

Conversation 1

1. Where is the conversation taking place?
   a) someone's home
   b) a boutique
   c) a big store

2. The present that the man will buy
   a) is too cheap for the occasion.
   b) costs no more than 20 pounds.
   c) is more expensive than he had expected.

Conversation 2

3. The man is
   a) a ski trainer.
   b) a friend of the woman.
   c) the woman's husband.

4. How does the woman feel?
   a) nervous
   b) enthusiastic
   c) disappointed

Conversation 3

5. What is the relationship between the two speakers?

   a) two friends

   b) husband and wife

   c) psychologist and patient

6. The woman is annoyed with the man because

   a) she thinks he doesn't help his wife around the house enough.

   b) she's worried that his kids aren't getting proper care.

   c) she thinks he doesn't make enough money.

Listening Part 3

You will hear someone talking. You will hear the person twice. Complete the information. Write short answers of one to five words.

Football Clinic

1. Next we will split:
   ....

2. Group A will work on:
   ....

3. Passing reduces the risk of:
   ....

4. Ball control will improve:
   ....

5. Location of restaurants:
   ....

6. Time to be back from lunch break:
   ....

7. What to do after lunch:
   ....

No.1 Practice Paper Tests

Listening Part 4

You will hear a conversation. You will hear the conversation twice. Choose the correct answers.

1. Who picked up the keys?
   a) no one
   b) the man
   c) the woman

2. The woman wants to keep the white couch because
   a) she doesn't want to carry it.
   b) it is comfortable.
   c) she can't afford a new one.

3. How much is rent at the man and woman's new place per month?
   a) 400 pounds
   b) 50 pounds
   c) 650 pounds

4. Why does the woman say the new place is more expensive?
   a) It is for two people, not one.
   b) Tim and Brad will be living there.
   c) Rent is split between three people.

5. The man thinks they must buy new furniture because
   a) he wants to get rid of his stuff.
   b) he wants to get rid of the woman's stuff.
   c) he wants them both to get rid of some of their stuff.

6. What time does the man think they must be at the estate agent's by?

   a) 9:15

   b) 1:00

   c) 12:00

Reading Part 1

Read the text and the questions. Choose the correct answer for each question.

THE WORKHOUSE: RELIEF FOR THE POOR?

The Oxford Dictionary's first record of the word "workhouse" dates back to 1652; however, workhouses were around even before that. State-provided help for the poor is often thought to have begun at the end of Queen Elizabeth's reign in 1601 when the passing of an Act for the Relief of the Poor made towns legally responsible for looking after their own poor people.

Relief was first given, in the form of money, clothing, food, or fuel, to poor people living in their own homes. However, the workhouse gradually began to evolve in the seventeenth century as an alternative form of help for poor people, both to save the town money, and also to make it a less pleasant option for healthy strong people who were able to work. In the workhouse, those who were able were required to work, usually without pay, in return for their board and lodging. The passing of the Workhouse Test Act in 1723, gave towns the option of denying other help to the poor and offering them only the prospect of the workhouse.

The threat of the workhouse was intended to discourage the able-bodied pauper from asking for help from the town. This was a principle of the "workhouse test" - help would only be given to those desperate enough to face entering the awful conditions of the workhouse. If an able-bodied man entered the workhouse, his whole family had to enter with him.

Life inside the workhouse was intended to be as off-putting as possible. Men, women, children, the sick and the able-bodied were housed separately. Families were separated. Parents were only allowed limited contact with their children; perhaps for an hour or so a week on Sunday afternoons. The elderly and the unwell sat around in the day rooms or sick-wards with little opportunity for visitors. The able-bodied were given hard work, such as stone breaking. Food was basic and monotonous: watery porridge called *gruel*, or bread and cheese. All inmates had to wear the rough workhouse uniform and sleep in crowded dormitories. Supervised baths were given once a week.

By the 1850s, the majority of those forced into the workhouse were not the lazy, but instead the old, the weak, the orphaned, unmarried mothers, and the physically or mentally ill. For the next century, the Union Workhouse was in many localities one of the largest and most significant buildings in the area, the largest ones accommodating more than a thousand inmates. Entering the workhouse was considered the ultimate degradation.

1. How did the towns first help the poor?
    a) by giving them things like money or food
    b) by building a large number of workhouses
    c) by giving them homes of their own

2. Why did towns prefer workhouses?
    a) It was better for the poor.
    b) It made them rich.
    c) It saved money.

3. Families
    a) were seldom allowed to enter workhouses.
    b) living in workhouses worked side by side.
    c) living in workhouses saw each other very rarely.

4. Those living in workhouses ate
   a) quite well most of the time.
   b) the same food almost every day.
   c) not enough to survive.

5. The inmates had
   a) very little privacy.
   b) to bathe every day.
   c) their own bedrooms.

6. The author of the text
   a) probably spent time in a workhouse.
   b) is celebrating the history of the workhouse.
   c) seems to view the workhouses negatively.

Reading Part 2

Read the text. Use the sentences to complete the text. Choose the correct sentence for each gap. There is one extra sentence you will not need.

Corsica

Corsica is the fourth largest island in the Mediterranean Sea, after Sicily, Sardinia and Cyprus. It is located west of Italy, southeast of the French mainland, and north of the island of Sardinia.

The island has an area of 8,682 sq km, and the island is mostly mountainous. **1**___ Ajaccio, the capital, and Bastia are the chief towns and ports. It has a population of around three hundred thousand.

Corsica was once an independent republic, but it became part of France in 1768. **2**___ The island is divided into two administrative departments. French is the official language of the island. **3**___ Although Corsica is considered one of the 26 regions of France, strictly speaking, it is designated as a "territorial collectivity" by law. As a territorial collectivity, it enjoys greater powers than other French regions, but for the most part its status is quite similar.

Much of the island is wild, covered by dense shrubs called *maquis*, whose flowers produce a fragrance that carries far out to sea. **4**___ The maquis also long provided hideouts for bandits, and banditry was not suppressed until the 1930s. Fruit, cork, cigarettes, wine and cheese are the main exports of the island. **5**___

Corsica is famed as the birthplace of Napoleon Bonaparte. His ancestral home, Casa Bonaparte, survives to this day. Many tourists come to Corsica simply to see the famed place he was originally from. Corsica has exceptionally good air and sea transport from continental France. It also has more than 200 beaches. **6**___

A. But, in 1077, Pope Gregory VII ceded Corsica to Pisa.

B. The largest mountain on the island is called Monte Cinto.

C. For all of these reasons, tourism is very important there.

D. Also, wheat is produced and sheep are raised.

E. This flower has earned Corsica the name "the scented isle".

F. However, most Corsicans also speak a dialect akin to Italian.

G. It is now considered a region of metropolitan France.

Reading Part 3

Read the four texts. Which text gives you the answer to each question? Choose the correct text (A-D) for each question.

A.

When deciding what to wear to ballet class, keep the following in mind: comfort and simplicity. The clothes you wear to practise ballet must allow you to move and stretch easily. Your clothing must also be tight enough for your teacher to check your body alignment during certain movements. Keep in mind that most ballet teachers prefer dancers to wear a cover-up of some sort to and from the studio. This is as simple as a pair of dance pants or a dance skirt paired with a crossover sweater or a sweatshirt worn over your leotard. Also, never use your ballet shoes as street shoes. Slip on a pair of sneakers or flip-flops instead, in order to prolong the life of your ballet shoes.

B.

There will be a dance contest on May 5th at the Bayfield Country Club. Please prepare a 3-minute dance routine and bring your own music. Contestants will be judged on creativity, technical skill and overall performance.

In each age group (5-10, 11-15, 16-20) there will be first, second and third-place prizes.

All dance styles are welcome.

C.

I have some very exciting news. Do you remember Mrs. Antrim, our old ballet teacher? Well, it turns out she's back in town and offering hip-hop classes! I know you've been looking for a new activity and I think hip-hop would be perfect! I'm definitely signing up for her beginners' class, so let me know if you want to sign up, too. I really think you should!

(The class costs 100 pounds for three months).

D.

Jazz dancing has evolved from two different eras in American history. Influenced by African-American dance, the earliest forms of jazz dance developed between 1800 and 1900. Since then Broadway choreographers have taken it to new places. In the 50's, when jazz was the main style of both dance and music, tap dance was the most popular form of jazz dance. As the era progressed new dances began to take form such as the Cakewalk, Charleston and Lindy Hop. Tap dance became more of a style of its own, as modern jazz dancing began to evolve. It is considered a very difficult dance to attain mastery in, but, with work, persistence and these videos you will be that much closer.

Which text

1. offers advice? ☐
2. is making a suggestion to someone? ☐
3. is a notice about an event? ☐

Which text provides the answers to the following questions?

4. Where did jazz dancing originate? ☐

5. How much does a class cost? ☐

6. How will people be judged? ☐

7. What should one wear to and from ballet class? ☐

Reading Part 4

Read the text and answer the questions. Use a maximum of five words for each question.

Honey for Your Cough

Coughs, sniffles, sneezes, runny noses. Colds and other nasty lung infections are especially common in winter. To fight the misery, many people swallow syrups and pills that claim to clear stuffy noses, soothe sore throats, stifle coughs and improve sleep.

Growing evidence, however, suggests that these medicines don't really work. What's worse, they can have unpleasant, even dangerous, side-effects, especially for young children. That's why some doctors are now recommending an ancient remedy for their coughing patients: honey.

It's the kind of advice you might expect from your grandmother. But a new study suggests that the sticky sweet stuff might have real healing power. "Honey has been used for centuries in folk remedies by cultures all over the world", says Ian Paul, a pediatrician at Pennsylvania State University Children's Hospital in Hershey, Pa.

Paul was motivated to test honey because treating coughs in children has recently become a sticky subject. Coughing is the body's way of clearing irritated airways to help you breathe. But too much coughing can make it tough to get the sleep your body needs to heal. Hoping to ease the suffering of their children, parents often give them cough medicine.

Most people think of honey as a tasty substitute for sugar in their tea, or as a topping on a peanut-butter-and-banana sandwich. So what gives the sweet stuff its healing powers? "For one thing, its thick, sticky consistency probably helps coat and soothe the throat", says Katherine Beals, a registered dietician at the University of Utah in Salt Lake City. She's also a nutrition consultant for the National Honey Board. "Substances called antioxidants may also be part of the answer", Beals says. Antioxidants, which are also found in foods such as blueberries, spinach, and dark chocolate, protect our cells from damage. Studies show that antioxidant levels in the body rise after someone swallows honey. All honey contains antioxidants, but certain types contain more than others.

"There are more than 300 types of honey", Beals says. Colour, flavour, and health benefits depend on which types of flowers honey-producing bees visit. "Most of the honey we buy in U.S. grocery stores is made by bees that visit clover plants. Darker honeys, such as the buckwheat type that Paul used in his experiment, are generally higher in antioxidants than lighter ones, including clover", Beals says.

Honey has another health advantage: at least some types seem to kill infectious microbes. One honey from New Zealand has proved especially good at healing wounds when slathered on the skin. "There is no evidence that eating honey will help prevent colds", Beals says. But if your throat is sore and you can't stop coughing, it might make you feel better. And a little dose of sweetness might just cheer you up!

No.1 Practice Paper Tests

1. What do modern people typically do when they get a cold?

   ....

2. Why do people cough when they're sick?

   ....

3. How does honey's consistency help someone who is sick?

   ....

4. What are two foods that have antioxidants?

   ....

5. What happens to someone's antioxidant levels when he swallows honey?

   ....

6. How many types of honey are there?

   ....

7. Where was honey found that was good for healing cuts?

   ....

Writing Part 1

Write a **letter** for an online magazine, in order to enter the competition advertised in the notice below.

In your **letter** you should:

- give several examples of things young people do for fun
- explain why they enjoy these activities
- explain how they benefit from these activities

Write between 100 and 150 words.

Today's Young and Furious! COMPETITION

We know how our readers love to have fun. We would like to find out how you and young people bring fun into your lives. Enter our competition by writing a short letter, telling us what you and your generation gets up to in their spare time.

Entries should be addressed to J. Browning, Young and Furious Competition, 12 Orchard Avenue, Middlesex, UK.

_____

_____

_____

_____

No.1 Practice Paper Tests

Writing Part 2

You are spending the summer in a foreign country. Write a text that you will post on **Facebook**, for your friends back home, suggesting they should also visit this country, either on holiday or in order to work there. In your text explain why you decided to go abroad and say what you like and dislike about where you are.

Write between 150 and 200 words.

No.1 Practice Paper Tests

LanguageCert
Communicator B2
Level 1
International ESOL (Listening, Reading, Writing)
Practice Paper Test 3

Listening Test Audio

Candidate's name (block letters please)

Centre no　　　　　　　　　　　**Date**

Time allowed:

Listening　　　　　　　　about 30 minutes

Reading and Writing　　　2 hours and 10 minutes

Instructions to Candidates

- An Answer Sheet will be provided.

- All answers must be transferred to the Answer Sheet.

- Please use a softpencil (2B, HB).

Listening Part 1

You will hear some short conversations. You will hear each conversation twice. Choose the correct answer for each conversation.

1. a) I'll try my best.
   b) Soon, I promise.
   c) No, I don't think so.

2. a) Oh, I thought it was the 17th!
   b) No, no! You were right the first time.
   c) I don't think you understood.

3. a) It doesn't surprise me.
   b) I'm positive; relax!
   c) You need to worry a bit.

4. a) I'm sure he'll be right back.
   b) I think his name was Tom.
   c) You're right; he's at the meeting.

5. a) Did it really?
   b) I bet you will.
   c) I don't know.

6. a) If they are, I'm not going.
   b) I haven't bought any tickets.
   c) Only if you're really sure.

7. a) It should be on the top left of the screen.
   b) Don't worry, it's easy.
   c) Double click on it.

Listening Part 2

You will hear some conversations. You will hear each conversation twice. Choose the correct answers for each conversation.

Conversation 1

1. The conversation is taking place at
   a) a small boutique.
   b) a department store.
   c) the woman's home.

2. In the end the woman
   a) goes to a department store.
   b) decides to shop online.
   c) gets a dress from a boutique.

Conversation 2

3. What is the relationship between the man and the woman?
   a) husband and wife
   b) friends
   c) siblings

4. The man and woman decide
   a) to go to the man's mother's house for their holiday.
   b) to stay at an amusement park for a week.
   c) to spend their holiday camping.

Conversation 3

5. What is the relationship between the two speakers?
   a) neighbours
   b) husband and wife
   c) mayor and citizen

6. Tom is
   a) the male speaker.
   b) the woman's son.
   c) the woman's husband.

Listening Part 3

You will hear someone talking. You will hear the person twice. Complete the information. Write short answers of one to five words.

Brookfield School's Field Day

1. The first Olympics could be called the first:
   ....

2. When to begin warm-up:
   ....

3. Duration of light physical activity:
   ....

4. Keen students can train for:
   ....

5. Maximum number of events to compete in:
   ....

6. Where to relax after the competition:
   ....

7. Location for the awards ceremony:
   ....

Listening Part 4

> You will hear a conversation. You will hear the conversation twice. Choose the correct answers.

1. What size dog does the man want at first?

    a) big

    b) small

    c) medium

2. The man's argument against small dogs is that

    a) they aren't cuddly.

    b) they can't protect the house.

    c) there isn't enough room in the house.

3. The woman tells the story about the dog biting her nose in order

    a) to show why she's afraid of big dogs.

    b) to entertain the man.

    c) to explain why she likes dogs.

4. What was the woman doing when she was bitten by the dog?

    a) buying things

    b) eating a cookie

    c) teasing the dog

5. The man thinks it is strange that the woman loves dogs because

    a) she is usually scared of things.

    b) he thinks she should like cows.

    c) she once had a bad experience with a dog.

6. What did the man hear about male dogs?
   a) They behave better than female dogs.
   b) They're cheaper.
   c) They're cute.

Reading Part 1

Read the text and the questions. Choose the correct answer for each question.

AN AUTUMN GAME

Conkers is a playground game traditionally played in September and October by children in Britain, the Republic of Ireland and some former British colonies using the seeds of horse-chestnut trees. The name 'conker' is also used for the seed and the tree itself. The horse-chestnut tree is not native to Britain, however, but was brought from the Balkans in the late 16th century. It was not widely planted until the early 19th century. Previously, children played with snail shells or hazelnuts.

To prepare for the game, a hole is drilled in a large, hard conker using a nail, gimlet, or small screwdriver. A piece of string, about 25cm long, is threaded through it. Often, a shoelace is used. A large knot at one or both ends of the string secures the conker.

The game is played between two people, each with a conker. They take turns hitting each other's conker using their own. One player lets the conker dangle on the full length of the string while the other player swings their conker in an effort to strike their opponent's. They take turns trying to strike each other's conker until one breaks. When this happens, the player whose conker remains intact gains a point. This may be either the attacking player or (more often) the defending one.

A new conker is a 'none-er' meaning that it has conquered none yet. If a none-er breaks another none-er then it becomes a one-er; if it was a 'one-er' then it becomes a two-er, and so on. If the defeated conker had accumulated points from previous wins, the winner takes the points of the defeated conker, as well as gaining a point for winning that particular game. For example, if a two-er plays a three-er, the surviving conker will become a six-er.

The hardest conkers usually win. Hardening conkers is often done by keeping them for a year, baking them briefly, soaking or boiling them in vinegar, or painting them with clear nail varnish. Such hardening is, however, usually regarded as cheating. Another factor affecting the strength of a conker is the shape of the hole; a clean cylindrical hole is stronger, as it has no notches that can begin a crack or split.

In 1965 the World Conker Championships were set up in Ashton, Northamptonshire, England, and still take place on the second Sunday of October every year. In 2014, an audience of 5,600 turned up to watch more than 500 competitors from all over the world.

1. How is the conker kept on the string?
    a) with a nail
    b) with a large knot
    c) with a shoelace

2. The game requires
    a) two players and a conker.
    b) two players and two conkers.
    c) any number of people and a conker.

3. How do you win the game?
    a) You hit the other conker.
    b) You break your conker.
    c) You break the other conker.

4. Winners may earn
   a) their opponent's conker.
   b) one point in each game.
   c) different numbers of points.

5. What is NOT considered cheating?
   a) soaking the conker in vinegar
   b) drilling a hole in your conker
   c) baking the conker

6. What is true of the game of conkers?
   a) It is still popular today.
   b) It is costly.
   c) It is losing its popularity.

Reading Part 2

Read the text. Use the sentences to complete the text. Choose the correct sentence for each gap. There is one extra sentence you will not need.

The Tower Of London

Her Majesty's Royal Palace and Fortress, more commonly known as the 'Tower of London', and in the past as simply 'The Tower', is a historic monument in central London, England, on the north bank of the River Thames. It is located within the London Borough of Tower Hamlets.

The term 'Tower of London' is often associated with the White Tower, the original stark square fortress section built by William the Conqueror in 1078. **1** Some are preserved very well, even today.

Throughout its history, it has served many different functions. The tower functioned primarily as a fortress, a royal palace and a prison. **2** The future Queen Elizabeth I was one of the most famous of these. This use of the tower as a prison has led to the phrase 'sent to the Tower', **3** The tower has also served as a place of execution and torture, an armoury, a treasury, a zoo, the Royal Mint, a public records office and an observatory. It is also rumoured to be home to many ghosts. **4**

Today the Tower of London is principally a tourist attraction. The tower is manned by the Yeomen Warders (known as *Beefeaters*), who act as tour guides and provide security. **5** Every evening, the warders participate in the Ceremony of the Keys. In this ceremony, the Tower is secured for the night. **6**

A. They have become a tourist attraction in their own right.

B. However, the tower as a whole is a complex of several buildings.

C. Since 1303, it has housed the Crown Jewels of the United Kingdom.

D. The prison was used to house high-class and royal criminals in particular.

E. Many consider a trip to London incomplete without a visit to the Tower.

F. This means 'to be imprisoned'.

G. This supposed Roman origin is a myth.

Reading Part 3

Read the four texts. Which text gives you the answer to each question? Choose the correct text (A-D) for each question.

A.

Our company, PlayTime, has been committed to enriching childhood through play since 1929. This requires more than just creating playground equipment; it requires having an understanding of what it takes to allow children to discover and develop, while at the same time having fun. Over the last 80 years, we have firmly established ourselves as the global leader in commercial play equipment.

Our mission is to continue to be an industry leader, using our rotational moulding expertise, creative design engineering and manufacturing, dedicated employees and outstanding customer-focused service.

B.

Boundless Playgrounds is the first national non-profit organisation dedicated to helping communities create extraordinary barrier-free playgrounds where children, with and without disabilities, can develop essential skills for life as they learn together through play.

Amy Jaffe Barzach and her husband decided to create a playground where children with and without disabilities could play and learn together. After the playground opened in 1996, hundreds of people wanted to know how they could set up their own. This led a passionate team of parents and professionals to establish *Boundless Playgrounds* in 1997.

C.

Hi you! How are things? I'm writing to ask if you would like to help out with a project in town. We're recruiting volunteers to help build a new town playground in September.

Last year more than 25 children were hurt because the playground is unsafe but now we've raised enough money for new equipment. We just need more people to help make this dream a reality.

Write back or call if you're available any day in September to help out. Thank you so much!

D.

In the words of our four-year-old: 'Mummy, this park is cool'. She's right; the Glover playground really is fabulous.

The playground caters for all ages. On one side of the park are toddler swings, a nice sandpit with scoop digger and a little climbing structure for the toddlers.

In the centre you'll find a helicopter and a wonderful spinning circle kids can sit or lie on. There's also a magnificent framework of climbing walls. I can't possibly do this structure justice; you'll just have to go and see it.

Which text

1. is a request? ☐
2. is trying to promote something? ☐
3. is about a non-commercial organisation? ☐

Which text provides the answers to the following questions?

4. Where can you take your toddler so that they have fun?

5. When does the town need volunteers?

6. How long has the playground-building company been around?

7. Where can you find a spinning piece of playground equipment?

Reading Part 4

Read the text and answer the questions. Use a maximum of five words for each question.

Science Games

Daniel Kunkle spent most of his time in graduate school playing with a colourful puzzle called a Rubik's Cube. With clever computer programming, Kunkle figured out that any Rubik's Cube can be solved in 26 moves or fewer. The previous record was 27. Studying puzzles and games may sound like fun, and not like serious science, but the work might also eventually help scientists solve real-world problems.

Each side of a Rubik's Cube is divided into nine squares, like a tic-tac-toe board. When the puzzle is solved, all nine squares on each side are the same colour as one another. So, there's a red side, a green side, and so on. A series of random rotations mixes up the colours. To solve the puzzle, you have to make the right series of twists to group the same colours together again on each side. The Rubik's Cube can be arranged in about 43 quintillion possible ways. That's 43 with 18 zeros after it! By hand, it can take a long time to find a solution.

A computer can try every possible move and compare solutions to solve the problem much more quickly. But with so many potential arrangements, even the world's fastest computer would take a few weeks to come up with a solution. But Kunkle came up with ways to shorten the process and eventually set a new record of 26 steps to solve the Rubik's Cube. Researchers suspect the absolute minimum could be just 20 moves, but they have yet to prove it.

The strategies that Kunkle used to solve the cube can be applied to other complicated problems, especially ones that require you to search through lots of possibilities. Scheduling airplane flights to carry millions of people to a variety of destinations as quickly as possible is one example.

Jonathan Schaeffer of the University of Alberta in Edmonton, Canada, faced an even bigger challenge: winning at checkers. On a traditional checkerboard, each player starts with 12 pieces in his or her own back three rows. During each turn, players slide one piece a distance of one square toward their opponent's side. An enemy piece is captured by jumping your piece over it. The player that removes all enemy pieces wins.

Schaeffer's computer programme considered all possible moves and countermoves in a game of checkers. In spite of his efforts to cut down time, the computers took 18 years to finish the problem. In the end, it concluded that if neither player makes a mistake, the game will always be a tie. Like the methods Kunkle developed for the Rubik's Cube, Schaeffer's strategies are being applied to practical problems in scheduling. Indeed, it just goes to show that playing games can sometimes turn into serious science!

No.1 Practice Paper Tests

1. What is a Rubik's Cube?

....

2. What could studying puzzles and games lead to?

....

3. How long do people take to solve a Rubik's Cube?

....

4. How does the computer solve a Rubik's Cube?

....

5. How long would a very good computer take to solve a Rubik's Cube?

....

6. What real-world problem can be solved using Kunkle's programme?

....

7. How do you capture an enemy piece in checkers?

....

Writing Part 1

Write an **article** in response to the notice below, which you read in your local newspaper. Make sure to include

- different examples of popular foods
- the origin of any recipes you may know
- if you like or dislike your local cuisine and why

Write between 100 and 150 words.

Local Cuisine

We are looking for articles about local cuisine in different countries or regions.

Describe what people in your area like to eat.

Mention any interesting facts you may know about the cuisine in your area.

Write to George Green, Chief Editor.

No.1 Practice Paper Tests

Writing Part 2

Write an **essay** for your college magazine entitled 'My favourite sport'. Describe your favourite sport and say why you like it more than other sports that are also popular in your country.

Write between 150 and 200 words.

LanguageCert
Communicator B2
Level 1
International ESOL (Listening, Reading, Writing)
Practice Paper Test 4

Listening Test Audio

Candidate's name (block letters please)

Centre no   **Date**

Time allowed:

Listening   about 30 minutes

Reading and Writing   2 hours and 10 minutes

Instructions to Candidates

- An Answer Sheet will be provided.

- All answers must be transferred to the Answer Sheet.

- Please use a softpencil (2B, HB).

Listening Part 1

> You will hear some short conversations. You will hear each conversation twice. Choose the correct answer for each conversation.

1. a) Where are we going shopping?
   b) But I've got no money.
   c) Oh, all right then.

2. a) Oh, I don't think so!
   b) That's not quite what I meant!
   c) Not exactly! See?

3. a) You've got a 20-minute wait.
   b) I'm afraid I don't have time now.
   c) That would be from platform 5.

4. a) Take your pullover off.
   b) Have you had it long?
   c) I'll close the window.

5. a) No, she didn't buy anything.
   b) Yes, as far as I could tell.
   c) She must have; she had no money.

6. a) I don't regret it in the least.
   b) Patience! I learned a great deal about patience!
   c) My annual salary was 20,000 pounds.

7. a) I haven't the slightest idea.

   b) I need to get my eyes tested.

   c) Have you checked on the table?

Listening Part 2

You will hear some conversations. You will hear each conversation twice. Choose the correct answers for each conversation.

Conversation 1

1. Why was the woman late?
   a) The flight was delayed.
   b) Her luggage didn't arrive.
   c) She lost her passport.

2. The woman now feels
   a) excited.
   b) relieved.
   c) tired.

Conversation 2

3. The two speakers are
   a) brother and sister.
   b) neighbours.
   c) colleagues.

4. What are they doing?
   a) complaining about a relative
   b) planning a night out
   c) planning a holiday

Conversation 3

5. What is the man's problem?

   a) He has lost his job.

   b) He doesn't like his boss.

   c) He is unsure how to do his job.

6. The woman thinks

   a) the man has made a mistake.

   b) the man should get a new job.

   c) the man is worrying unnecessarily.

Listening Part 3

You will hear someone talking. You will hear the person twice. Complete the information. Write short answers of one to five words.

Customer Announcement

1. Day for late-night shopping:

   ....

2. Some children's shoes available at:

   ....

3. Duration of offer for CDs:

   ....

4. What's after the face painting at 5pm:

   ....

5. There are many options for people who are:

   ....

6. Place to eat pizza and pasta:

   ....

7. Smoking is:

   ....

No.1 Practice Paper Tests

Listening Part 4

You will hear a conversation. You will hear the conversation twice. Choose the correct answers.

1. What was Emma like when she was a student?

    a) She already had an idea of what she wanted to do.

    b) Everyone thought she'd become a successful businesswoman.

    c) She always felt tired.

2. What stopped Emma from starting her own business as soon as she graduated?

    a) She needed a business partner.

    b) She had no idea what she wanted to do with her life.

    c) She didn't know how to go about starting her own business.

3. When Emma was 25

    a) she decided that she had to follow her dream.

    b) she started to make cakes for her friends.

    c) she found a nice house that she wanted to buy.

4. How did Emma feel about sharing a house?

    a) She was reluctant to live on her own.

    b) It made her feel as though she were underperforming in life.

    c) She got bored with doing all the cooking for everyone.

5. When Emma was a child

    a) she'd often accidently break eggs.

    b) she lived with her grandmother.

    c) she got satisfaction out of helping in the kitchen.

6. What advice does Emma give about starting your own business?

   a) You must be realistic.

   b) You must have a lot of money.

   c) You need to have a business partner.

Reading Part 1

Read the text and the questions. Choose the correct answer for each question.

It happened at night

Tom woke suddenly. Feeling the floor moving under his bed and hearing the sound of breaking glass, he knew he had to get out of his old house as quickly as was humanly possible. He soon had his dressing gown back on, found his slippers and made for the door. When this had last happened, he'd had others to worry about, too. Mary had since gone to a better place where no ground ever shook. On the other side of town, their only son, Tom junior, would now be gathering his wife, son and daughter and other valuables. No doubt he would want to save what he could if it turned out to be a big one. Reminiscences were a luxury he couldn't afford at that instant but the thought did occur to the old man that the son to whom he had given so much would not now be thinking of him.

The cold of the night, once he was out in the relative safety of the open street, made Tom wish he had planned his escape more calmly. If he had only stopped to think, he would have recalled that the weatherman had forecast a clear sky with temperatures well below the seasonal average. And why hadn't he opened the wardrobe where his heavy overcoat now hung uselessly? Mary would have. These thoughts, though, were interrupted by a second, more violent tremor, which shook the street in anger. No sooner had it passed than Tom found himself surrounded by equally frightened neighbours who normally would not even have said hello to him. Sad, lonely thoughts returned. Nothing like the threat of a natural disaster, Tom complained to himself, to bring people together!

Dawn broke eventually. By the light of the rising sun, it appeared that the buildings in Tom's street had suffered no structural damage at all. Strangely enough, he was more contented than he had been in years. A family in the flats next door had befriended him. He now stood chatting to the youngster who had lent him the warm leather jacket which he had put on over his dressing gown. The boy's mum had somehow made hot soup for them all and they had drunk out of mugs, standing around a fire that dad had lit in the middle of the road. The news that reached them from a group crowded around a car with its radio on was good; apparently no further major tremors were expected. The earthquake's epicentre had been under the sea two hundred kilometres away. It was safe to go back indoors.

Tom wondered whether others might not have been so lucky. He vowed to return the kindness he had been shown. What is more, he would stop feeling bitterly sorry for himself. From now on, he would swallow his pride and give Tom junior the chance to help him out now and again. All it would take was one phone call.

1. What can be understood about the man in this story?
    a) He had been living alone after his wife's death.
    b) His son had treated him unkindly.
    c) He had only recently become divorced.

2. The earthquake
    a) caused no real damage.
    b) started a fire in the man's street.
    c) was felt over a small area only.

3. We can suppose that before the earthquake Tom's neighbours
    a) had drawn the conclusion that he wanted to be left alone.
    b) disapproved of the way he treated his wife and children.
    c) were jealous of him because he lived in a house, not a flat.

4. Tom's attitude to himself and others
   a) was altered by his experiences that night.
   b) was left unchanged by the earthquake.
   c) worsened and became more bitter after the earthquake.

5. This story shows that
   a) old people should be cared for by their children.
   b) children can be ungrateful towards their parents.
   c) people are sometimes responsible for their own unhappiness.

6. Which one of the following did Tom most probably do first, later that day?
   a) buy a new leather jacket for the boy next door
   b) get in touch with a close relative of his
   c) invite his friendly neighbours to dinner to show his thanks

Reading Part 2

Read the text. Use the sentences to complete the text. Choose the correct sentence for each gap. There is one extra sentence you will not need.

Dreaming of Retirement?

It is a moment that millions dream of: waking up on the first day of retirement. Freed, at last, from the daily workload, to sip cold drinks in the garden, gently enjoy pastimes and hobbies, and explore exotic lands at leisure. That's the dream.

1 ____ It found that more than 50 percent of pensioners felt 'unhappy' on the first day of their retirement. About one in ten said they felt 'sad', 'anxious' or 'lost'. Only 48 per cent said they felt 'happy'.

A spokesman for the Department for Work and Pensions, which carried out the study, said employees are increasingly rejecting the traditional idea of retirement. **2** ____ Many would like to take a more gradual approach, slowly cutting back their hours or the number of days they work. Others just want to keep on working. **3** ____ At 65, people have suddenly got two or three decades facing them and wonder how to fill the time. Work is what they have been doing for as long as they can remember.

The DWP questioned about 1,000 men and women about how they felt on the first day of their retirement. **4** ____ The most common answer was 'friends', followed by 'being challenged', 'office humour and gossip' and 'a reason to get out of the house'. **5** ____

Yet, official figures show the number of pensioners working beyond state pension age has increased by more than 55 per cent to 1.3 million. And for many of those still working, it is a necessity. **6** ____

A. They were also asked what they missed about their jobs.

B. Holidays were said to be their main interest.

C. But the reality is very different, a report reveals today.

D. With just a basic state pension, many cannot afford to retire.

E. People seem reluctant to suddenly stop full-time work at 60 or 65.

F. Some of the reasons are financial, but it is not only about money.

G. Others missed the office party, dressing smartly, or the canteen.

Reading Part 3

Read the four texts. Which text gives you the answer to each question? Choose the correct text (A-D) for each question.

A.

I hope you are well. No doubt Mum and Dad told you I ended up in Nairobi with no luggage as they forgot to put it on the plane! I only had the clothes I was wearing. All my mountain climbing gear was in my rucksack. Still, I was able to borrow and hire clothes and equipment for the climb and I actually made it to the top. Can you believe it? I felt really proud of myself.

Anyway, my bag was waiting for me when I got back to Nairobi.

Miss everyone!
Lots of love!

B.

As I discussed with you last week, please find enclosed copies of my plane ticket, passport and insurance claim from British Airways confirming that my luggage was late arriving in Nairobi and that I therefore had to pay extra money to hire and buy clothes and equipment.

I have included all the information that you have requested so I hope that my claim can be dealt with as quickly as possible as I am depending on the extra expenses being refunded in order to be able to finance the rest of my trip.

C.

British Airways booking confirmation

Passenger name: Jenny Sarah Abbot

Flight: BA 697 from London Heathrow to Nairobi

Departure time: 06:30, from Terminal 5

Arrival time: 17:00

Please ensure that you check in two hours before departure. All luggage should be clearly labelled and locked. Maximum weight for luggage is 25 kg per passenger plus one piece of hand luggage.
We recommend that you take out travel insurance for all flights.
See our website for special offers.

D.

A local girl, Jenny Abbot, has raised over £1000 for charity by climbing Mount Kilimanjaro in Kenya. But Jenny had to climb the mountain without her boots due to a problem with her luggage at Heathrow Airport. Jenny's bag arrived in Nairobi nearly a week later, after Jenny had climbed to the summit of the mountain. Jenny's mother, Samantha, said: "Naturally, Jenny was very upset when she realised that her luggage had gone missing, but she is very resourceful and she borrowed some equipment and hired some boots which enabled her to do what she was dreaming of since she was a kid." Jenny is due to return home next month.

Which text

1. was written after a conversation on the phone? ☐
2. was written by a journalist? ☐
3. gives advice? ☐

Which text provides the answers to the following questions?

4. Why did Jenny climb Mount Kilimanjaro? ☐
5. Why does Jenny need to have some money sent to her? ☐
6. How did Jenny feel at the top of the mountain? ☐
7. How much luggage was Jenny allowed to take to Kenya? ☐

Reading Part 4

Read the text and answer the questions. Use a maximum of five words for each question.

The law of the land

There are two distinct systems of law in Britain: one governing England and Wales, and one governing Scotland. Both systems have their own court structures, but they are alike in having separate courts for criminal and civil law. Generally speaking, criminal law is concerned with wrongs against the country; civil law with disputes between private individuals. The main purpose of the criminal court is to punish, while that of the civil court is to compensate, usually financially.

The criminal courts

Ninety percent of all criminal cases in the English system are dealt with in the 900 or so Magistrates' Courts. Generally, these are less serious crimes. More serious crimes, such as murder, may be sent to the Crown Court for trial by judge and jury if there is enough evidence. Most magistrates are unpaid and without legal qualifications, but in some of the larger cities there are professional magistrates who are paid. These paid magistrates make decisions alone, whereas most magistrates make decisions in groups of three.

The Magistrates' Courts have their origins in 1195, when 'Knights of the Peace' were first created; their duties were essentially to keep the law and act as police officers. These duties slowly evolved until 1361, when the first 'Justice of the Peace' was appointed; in other words, the first magistrate.

The Crown Courts not only deal with more serious crimes but also handle appeals against magistrates' decisions. On a plea of not guilty, a case in a Crown Court will be heard by a judge, whose job is to interpret and explain the law and pass the sentence. But the guilt or innocence of the accused is decided not by the judge, but by a jury of twelve carefully-chosen people.

The civil courts

There are about 330 civil courts, which date in their modern form from 1846, when they were established to deal quickly and cheaply with smaller claims. A large amount of their work is connected to property issues and divorce. Cases are usually decided by a judge alone but small claims are settled by a registrar.

The history of the superior civil courts is extremely complicated. Today, there are three divisions of the High Court: the Family Division, dealing with marriages and children; the Chancery Division, concerned with money and property; and the Queen's Bench Division, which handles most other cases.

Other courts

Old English law had many other small courts which no longer exist. One older court that still exists is the Coroner's Court. As well as investigating suspicious deaths, the coroner can also investigate any fires that happen in London.

No.1   Practice Paper Tests

1. What does the civil court usually do?

....

2. Where would the most serious crimes be tried?

....

3. What can paid magistrates do that others cannot?

....

4. What was the main job of the Knights of the Peace?

....

5. In a Crown Court, who decides if someone is guilty?

....

6. What does a registrar deal with?

....

7. Who would decide if someone died in a strange way?

....

Writing Part 1

Write a **review** about a book for a language magazine for learners of English, as requested in the notice below.

Mention:

- what the book was about
- how it made you feel
- if you would recommend it to others or not

Write between 100 and 150 words.

Modern English Language Learner Magazine

'A good book can touch your heart'

Fewer people today are reading books. We would like to encourage people to start reading again by getting our readers to review a book that affected them in some way. The best reviews will be published in next month's magazine.

Send your review to:

Amanda Scott,

The Modern English Language Learner Magazine

10, The Broadwalk, Essex, UK.

No.1 Practice Paper Tests

Writing Part 2

Write a **letter** to your Australian pen friend and tell them about the area where you live. Say what you like and what you dislike most about your village, town or city.

Write between 150 and 200 words.

No.1 Practice Paper Tests

LanguageCert
Communicator B2
Level 1
International ESOL (Listening, Reading, Writing)
Practice Paper Test 5

Listening Test Audio

Candidate's name (block letters please)

Centre no   **Date**

Time allowed:

Listening   about 30 minutes

Reading and Writing   2 hours and 10 minutes

Instructions to Candidates

- An Answer Sheet will be provided.

- All answers must be transferred to the Answer Sheet.

- Please use a softpencil (2B, HB).

Listening Part 1

You will hear some short conversations. You will hear each conversation twice. Choose the correct answer for each conversation.

1. a) I'm sorry, I must have missed it.
   b) Why, thank you; I'm glad to hear it.
   c) What did you want to know?

2. a) Turn left at the second intersection.
   b) No, I think you'd better hurry.
   c) It is a bit of a walk.

3. a) Eat it yourself, then.
   b) Well, who do you think it was?
   c) Well, I'm afraid you're mistaken.

4. a) You look great in both.
   b) You don't give me any choice then.
   c) Yes, it's much nicer.

5. a) I don't agree, actually.
   b) Yes, I agree.
   c) I had no idea.

6. a) Well, I can't see a sign anywhere.
   b) You don't say!
   c) I haven't got a cigarette.

7. a) Don't tempt me!
   b) How can you say that!
   c) It's complicated; I'm not sure.

Listening Part 2

You will hear some conversations. You will hear each conversation twice. Choose the correct answers for each conversation.

Conversation 1

1. The woman wants a computer because
   a) she needs it for her job.
   b) she wants to be able to email people.
   c) she needs it to get a better job.

2. Why does the woman decide to choose the laptop?
   a) It looks attractive.
   b) It comes with a nice table.
   c) It is cheap and easy to store.

Conversation 2

3. The two speakers are
   a) aunt and nephew.
   b) neighbours.
   c) husband and wife.

4. Why are they unhappy about the situation?
   a) They won't be able to have a holiday.
   b) The woman doesn't enjoy the job she is doing.
   c) They wanted more money to pay for something they were planning.

Conversation 3

5. What is the man's problem?

   a) He is going to be late for an appointment.

   b) He missed his important business meeting.

   c) He is nervous about a meeting.

6. The woman will

   a) cancel her business meeting.

   b) call a taxi.

   c) phone the dentist.

Listening Part 3

You will hear someone talking. You will hear the person twice. Complete the information. Write short answers of one to five words.

Recorded Message from Cinema World

1. Many benefits for:
   ....

2. E-newsletter sent straight to your:
   ....

3. Deadline for making a reservation:
   ....

4. 'Death in the Woods' not suitable for:
   ....

5. End of the 'New Wave' Festival on:
   ....

6. For a discount, buy Festival tickets at:
   ....

7. Advertised programmes, online at:
   ....

No.1 Practice Paper Tests

Listening Part 4

You will hear a conversation. You will hear the conversation twice. Choose the correct answers.

1. What is surprising about Margaret?
   a) She got married in her early thirties.
   b) She always wanted to be a teacher.
   c) She wasn't a good student at school.

2. Margaret decided to change her life because
   a) she didn't enjoy being a mother.
   b) she became a single mother.
   c) she wanted to leave her husband.

3. How did Margaret get involved with teaching children with special needs?
   a) Someone suggested she should try it.
   b) One of her own children went to a special needs school.
   c) She had always planned to be a special needs teacher.

4. When Margaret arrived at her first school
   a) she was shocked that the children weren't being cared for properly.
   b) she found it quite difficult to teach the children with special needs.
   c) she believed the children could achieve more than they were at the time.

5. The school motto could be described as
   a) pessimistic.
   b) depressing.
   c) positive.

6. What did the school do that was different from other special schools?

   a) They gave the children the chance to concentrate on academic subjects.

   b) They concentrated on design and technology.

   c) They only taught academic subjects.

Reading Part 1

Read the text and the questions. Choose the correct answer for each question.

All work and no play

The street was poorly lit, which suited the man who had just entered the tall, steel and glass building. Everything was quiet, just as he had foreseen it would be, apart from the humming noise of a lone vacuum cleaner on one of the lower floors. As he climbed the stairs, he went through his plan one last time. Only a minor detail escaped him: would the cleaning lady be Alice or Jane? Alice, he remembered, was Monday and Wednesday; Jane, Tuesday and Thursday. But, who on earth was Friday? No matter, he thought; he'd just have to wait and see.

He reached the second floor and went straight to the office he now knew so well. Having let himself in, he walked soundlessly across the floor to the computer workstation next to the big desk. The monitor glowed welcomingly in the darkness. Upstairs, the carpets were still being cleaned. As long as he could hear that, he knew he could get on with his business undisturbed.

Seated, he examined the screen. He felt no surprise to read the message, 'Three hours, twenty minutes and thirty seconds. Please wait.' The night before, it had been even longer. The delay never failed to give him great pleasure. What he felt during it was a sense of his own power. How could he possibly feel anything of the kind when he served his boss his coffee or when he was sent out on an errand to deliver packages to complete strangers? Nobody really knew him at all. 'Three hours, twenty seven minutes and five seconds. Please wait.' He knew he had given the Russian something more than he'd bargained for. As the minutes passed, his confidence grew.

Then the reply was up there on the screen for his eyes to see: 'G6 - H8'. The meaning of this retreat was immediately understood. The Russian was on the defensive. He had seen the threat in Thursday's move. But the real damage had been done, unnoticed, as early as Monday. Brimming with confidence, the man in the quiet office typed his reply. What was the good of waiting? Better to get it over with before Alice, (or would it be Jane), arrived.

"Black resigns. New Game? Type Y for Yes, N for No". Before there was any time to answer, the door opened. All the lights came on. "Working late again, Humphrey?" a friendly voice asked. "That's three times this week! I hope your boss realises what a good boy you are." "Y," he said in his excitement as his right index finger hit the key. "You know very well why," the voice went on. "There aren't that many young men these days who'd be willing to come back after hours to make sure those awful computers are working properly, are there now?"

Humphrey did not contradict her. Before rising, he keyed in 'D2 - D4'. As he said good night, he cleared the screen.

1. Humphrey
    a) disliked his boss very much.
    b) was involved in an illegal activity.
    c) enjoyed taking part in certain kinds of competition.

2. It is likely that the Russian in the story
    a) was a close friend of Humphrey's.
    b) had met Humphrey but didn't know him very well.
    c) had never met Humphrey.

3. During the day, Humphrey probably
   a) kept quiet about coming back to the office after the others had left.
   b) spent most of his time sitting at his computer workstation.
   c) boasted to his colleagues about his successes.

4. What was Humphrey's reaction to the person who came in?
   a) He was excited.
   b) He hardly took any notice.
   c) He showed extreme dislike for her.

5. What mistake did a person in this story make?
   a) She or he misunderstood something that was said.
   b) She or he mistook somebody for somebody else.
   c) She or he got the days of the week mixed up.

6. Which of the following statements is true about Humphrey?
   a) He did a lot of overtime without getting paid for it.
   b) He had a high opinion of himself and found his job boring.
   c) He lacked self-confidence, which made his job difficult for him.

Reading Part 2

Read the text. Use the sentences to complete the text. Choose the correct sentence for each gap. There is one extra sentence you will not need.

Re-balance your mind

We each have our own personal energy vampires: people, anxieties and commitments that leave you without a moment for yourself. And although you can't get rid of them from your life entirely, there's plenty you can do to reduce the stress they create.

1 However, whether it's grief, anger or resentment, unexpressed emotions sap your energy and drain your happiness. So find a way to express your feelings. **2** Negative thoughts make you tired and anxious while positive ones give you a lift. So, work at re-thinking situations: make a conscious effort to seek out the positives in every situation. **3** Be aware of the things you feel pleased with yourself about and are grateful for, however small they may be.

We create a lot of stress through our own perfectionism but, in most cases, good enough really is good enough. The quest for perfection tends to be rooted in our own lack of self-esteem. **4** However, most people prefer to be around someone who doesn't do things perfectly and is more relaxed about life. So, congratulate yourself for the things you do well and accept your limitations with the rest.

Another way to fight stress it to cut back on your commitments. Make a list of all your responsibilities starting with the most essential and working downwards; then draw a line through the middle. **5** Things might not be done your way or as well as you would do them, but they will get done. This will give you some breathing space. **6**

A. Cancel, excuse yourself from or delegate everything below that line.

B. Always being on the go can become a way of avoiding difficult feelings.

C. If you always say 'Yes', you'll regret it.

D. End each day by writing down the good things that have happened.

E. It can also come from a fear of others judging us.

F. We make ourselves too important but it's important to share some of the responsibility, too.

G. Start a journal, or talk to a counsellor to help you through the process.

Reading Part 3

Read the four texts. Which text gives you the answer to each question? Choose the correct text (A-D) for each question.

A.

I am writing with reference to the cottage we rented from you. There were a number of problems which made our holiday less enjoyable. Firstly, we were very disappointed that the swimming pool hadn't been cleaned and so we couldn't use it. Also, your brochure said the cottage was an easy walk to the beach, but it took us half an hour and involved walking up a very steep hill. My wife has a bad back, so we had to take the car. We had a nice time anyway, but I feel that you should deal with these issues.

B.

I am very sorry to hear that you had some problems during your stay at our cottage. Unfortunately, the man who cleans our pool was sick that week and we did not realise because, as you know, we were away ourselves.

As far as the brochure is concerned, I agree that the information about the beach is misleading and I will change it. We did not know about your wife's condition, so we couldn't know the hill would be a problem, but I will mention it in our new brochure.

No.1 Practice Paper Tests

C.

Holidaylettings is the UK's fastest growing holiday home rental site. It enables holiday-home owners to market their property directly to holidaymakers, giving them more flexibility and control over how and when they let their property.

The site presents in-depth information on over 13,000 holiday homes in 80 countries worldwide. Once holidaymakers have found a suitable property, they simply contact the owner directly to arrange the booking.

Each advert includes up to 16 colour photographs, and an availability calendar, and costs just £99 per year, making this great value for money.

D.

Come and enjoy a family holiday at our beautiful cottage by the sea. Only a short walk to the beach, you can have a swim in the clean blue water or even go surfing.

Seaview Cottage has three bedrooms, a dining room, lounge, fully-equipped kitchen and two bathrooms. There is a heated outdoor swimming pool which is cleaned twice a week and a lovely sun patio next to the pool.

Seaview Cottage is available all year round at a cost of £600 per week.

For further information or reservations:
type in reference number 184935 on the holidaylettings website.

Which text

1. was written by a business?   ☐
2. mentions that something was not accurate?   ☐
3. mentions an important number?   ☐

LanguageCert Communicator CEFR Level B2 ESOL/SELT 朗思全真模拟题 1

Which text provides the answers to the following questions?

4. What health issues does someone have? ☐

5. How can you get more information? ☐

6. Who is going to edit some information? ☐

7. How often do you pay for something? ☐

No.1 Practice Paper Tests

Reading Part 4

Read the text and answer the questions. Use a maximum of five words for each question.

Britain: a nation of dieters?

Britain was branded a nation of failed serial dieters yesterday. Millions eagerly try every new weight-loss fad or fitness craze, but at least half give up after less than a month. A survey found that most blamed their failure on a lack of time or money. But the study suggested lack of willpower was a major factor.

The survey of 2,000 men and women - commissioned by Marks and Spencer - found losing weight was the most important thing on people's minds at the start of the year. Some 49 percent put it ahead of getting fit and making more money as a must for the year ahead. Waistlines were the biggest cause of concern, with almost 40% citing a slimmer tummy as the most important goal.

Yet, half of those asked admitted that it took less than a month for their willpower to crack, slipping back into unhealthy diets and eating lots of fattening treats. Chocolate was voted the hardest to resist, ahead of crisps and cheese. Four in ten blamed their failure on lack of cash to spend on gym membership and healthy foods. Almost as many said they simply did not have the time for food preparation and exercise.

The figures will make grim reading for government experts trying to stop the nation's obesity epidemic. Half of the adults in England are obese or overweight, while obesity in children has leapt 25 percent over the last 15 years, as they drink more and more fizzy drinks containing sugar and eat more and more junk food. This is serious since obesity cuts life expectancy by nine years, on average, and increases the risk of health problems such as heart disease, diabetes, stroke and some cancers.

Jenny Arthur, Marks and Spencer's food nutritionist, said: "People are fooled into believing they need to follow an expensive eating plan, swapping balanced meals for drink replacement meals or a meat-enriched diet such as Atkins diet. It's a misconception that healthy eating is time-consuming and expensive; there are a number of quick and easy options available, and a lot of the time it's more about watching what you eat and how much you eat. Dieters should set themselves achievable targets, and give themselves 'mini-rewards' when they reach a target. It also helps to find a friend who wants to lose weight and call them if you are feeling miserable. Another good idea is to write down all the reasons why you want to lose weight. This should be kept to hand for whenever temptation raises its head."

No.1 Practice Paper Tests

1. What is the real reason people don't diet successfully?

....

2. Who paid for the study?

....

3. What part of the body are people most worried about?

....

4. What has gone up by a quarter?

....

5. By how much might your life be shortened if you are very overweight?

....

6. What do people mistakenly believe healthy eating is?

....

7. When you achieve something what should you give yourself?

....

Writing Part 1

Write an **article** for a travel magazine as requested in the notice below, trying to convince readers of the magazine to visit the village, town or city you live in. Give details of the following:

- places of interest to visit
- any interesting history or tradition
- what makes this place unique

Write between 100 and 150 words.

The Place I Call Home

Today many people travel far and wide but we spend most of our lives in our own town because that's the place we love and feel good in. We would like to know what you like most about where you live and what makes it a good place to visit.

Send us an article entitled "the Place I Call Home".

Send your article to Ken Goddard, Magazine Editor.

The best articles will be published in the August edition of "Far and Wide".

No.1 Practice Paper Tests

Writing Part 2

Write a **narrative** for your school magazine entitled "A day that I learned something". Narrate what happened during a day when you experienced something important and explain why you believe that learning isn't accomplished only in school.

Write between 150 and 200 words.

No.2

Speaking Tests
ESOL

LanguageCert Communicator CEFR Level B2 ESOL/SELT 朗思全真模拟题 1

Test 1

Part 1 (3 minutes)

I: **Interlocutor, C: Candidate**

I: International Spoken ESOL Exam, Communicator Level, *(give today's date)*.

(Give candidate's name.) **Exam begins.**

Hello. My name's *(give full name)*. Can you spell your family name for me please?

C: *(Spells family name)*

I: Thank you. Which country are you from?

C: *(Responds)*

I: Thank you. Now, Part One. I'm going to ask you some questions about yourself and your ideas.

(Choose up to five questions, one from each of the different topic areas, as time allows. Name the topic; eg 'Now, Education.')

Topics

Education

- What is/was your favourite subject in school?
- What educational achievement are you most proud of?
- What is/was the most difficult subject for you in school? Why?
- Do/did you like or dislike school? Why or why not?

Local Area

- What is your favourite thing about your local area?
- What would you do to improve your local area?
- What is there to do around where you live?
- What is one reason people would like to move to your area?

Food

- What is your favourite food?

- ❏ What is your least favourite food?
- ❏ Tell me about a restaurant you like to eat at.
- ❏ What foreign foods have you tried?

Sport
- ❏ Do/did you play any sports?
- ❏ What is your favourite sport?
- ❏ Do you like watching sports?
- ❏ Do you think playing a sport is a good way to meet new people?

Future Plans
- ❏ What are your goals over the next few years?
- ❏ Where do you see yourself in ten years?
- ❏ What skills would you like to gain in the future?
- ❏ Tell me something about your future plans regarding work.

C: *(Responds.)*

I: *(Interlocutor makes brief responses and / or comments.)*

I: Thank you.

LanguageCert Communicator CEFR Level B2 ESOL/SELT 朗思全真模拟题 1

Part 2 (3 minutes)

I: Now, Part Two. We are going to role-play some situations. I want you to start or respond. First situation *(choose one situation from A)*.

A

- We're friends. I start.

  What are you doing after school tomorrow?

- I work at the doctor's office. You're feeling very sick. I start.

  Do you need to see the doctor right away?

- We work together. I start.

  Did you get the report written in time?

- We're friends. I start.

  I want to do something fun this weekend. Do you have any ideas?

C: *(Responds.)*

I: *(Role-play the situation with candidate - approximately two turns each.)*

I: Second situation. *(choose one situation from B)*.

B

- We're friends. You want me to look after your cat while you're away. You start.

- I'm your teacher. You haven't finished a homework assignment. You start.

- I am a waiter at a restaurant. You want to order. You start.

- I'm your boss. You're late for work. You start.

C: *(Initiates.)*

I: *(Role-play the situation with candidate - approximately two turns each.)*

I: *(Role-play a third situation from A or B if time allows.)*

I: Thank you.

No.2 Speaking Tests ESOL

Part 3 (3 minutes)

I: Now, Part Three. We're going to discuss something together.

We're planning a dance in town. Let's talk about what kind of dance we want to have and make some decisions. Here are some ideas. *(Hand over candidate's task sheet.)* I have some different ideas.

Take twenty seconds to think about what you want to say. *(20 seconds.)* Please start.

Interlocutor's Task Sheet

Town Dance

Place: Town Hall or City Park Centre

Food: Bring your own

Theme: "Celebrating History"

Music: Local bands

Time: Starts at 7 or 8, ends at 10 or 11

Candidate's Task Sheet

Town Dance

Place: School gymnasium or Town Hall

Food: none or light snacks

Theme: "Future Plans"

Music: Local DJ

Time: Starts at 9 or 10, ends whenever

I: Thank you. *(Retrieve candidate's task sheet.)*

No.2 Speaking Tests ESOL

Part 4 (4 minutes including follow-up questions)

I: In Part Four you are going to talk on your own for about two minutes. Your topic is *(choose topic for candidate)*.

Topics
A **The best party you've ever attended.**
B **Something interesting you've recently heard in the news.**
C **Your local community - things to do there, geography, people, places.**

I: You now have thirty seconds to write some notes to help you. *(Hand over piece of paper and pen/pencil.)* So your topic is *(repeat topic)*. *(Withdraw eye contact for thirty seconds. Leave recorder running.)*

I: *(Candidate's name)*, **please start.**

C: *(Talks.)*

I: *(When candidate has talked for a maximum of two minutes, say, 'Thank you', and then ask some follow-up questions.)*

Follow-up questions
The best party you've ever attended
- Where was it?
- What did you do there that made it great?
- What was the party celebrating?
- What specific memories do you have of the party?

Something interesting you've recently heard in the news
- Where did you hear this piece of news?
- Where do you typically get your news from?
- Is keeping up to date with current events important to you?
- What type of news do you find interesting?

Your local community - things to do there, geography, people, places
- What features about your community do you like best?
- How long have you lived in your community?
- What do you like least about your community?
- What is an outstanding feature of your community?

C: *(Responds.)*

I: Thank you, *(give candidate's name.)* **That is the end of the exam.**

No.2 Speaking Tests ESOL

Test 2

Part 1 (3 minutes)

I: International Spoken ESOL Exam, Communicator Level, *(give today's date)*. *(Give candidate's name.)* Exam begins.

Hello. My name's (*give full name*). Can you spell your family name for me please?

C: *(Spells family name.)*

I: Thank you. Which country are you from?

C: *(Responds.)*

I: Thank you. Now, Part One. I'm going to ask you some questions about yourself and your ideas.

(Choose up to five questions, one from each of the different topic areas, as time allows. Name the topic; eg 'Now, Your family.')

Topics

Your family

- How many people are in your family?
- How important is family to you?
- Name some things you enjoy doing with your family.
- How do you keep in touch with your family when you're apart?

Yourself

- What is your favourite colour?
- What do you like to do in your free time?
- What is your dream job?
- What is your favourite holiday?

Food

- Who normally cooks in your house?

- ❒ Have you ever cooked a meal that other people liked?
- ❒ Who is your favourite celebrity chef?
- ❒ Do you try to avoid food that contains a lot of fat?

Recent Experiences
- ❒ What is something exciting you've done in the past year?
- ❒ What is something new you've tried recently?
- ❒ What have you done this past year?
- ❒ Have you accomplished anything special recently?

Travel
- ❒ What travel experiences have you had?
- ❒ Is there a place that you have never been to?
- ❒ Where would you like to go to?
- ❒ Who do you prefer to travel with?
- ❒ Where is the best place you've travelled to?

C: *(Responds.)*

I: *(Interlocutor makes brief responses and/or comments.)*

I: Thank you.

Part 2 (3 minutes)

I: Now, Part Two. We are going to role-play some situations. I want you to start or respond. First situation *(choose one situation from A).*

A

- We're friends. I start.

    Are you busy tomorrow evening?

- I work at a restaurant. I start.

    Good evening. Are you ready to order?

- I am your boss. I start.

    Why were you so late for work this morning?

- We're friends. I start.

    What do you want to do for your birthday next week?

C: *(Responds.)*

I: *(Role-play the situation with candidate - approximately two turns each.)*

I: *Second situation. (choose one situation from B).*

B

- We're friends. You want to borrow my car. You start.

- I'm your doctor. You feel very sick. You start.

- I work in a clothes store. You want to buy a new shirt. You start.

- I'm a police officer. You hurt yourself and want my help. You start.

C: *(Initiates.)*

I: *(Role-play the situation with candidate - approximately two turns each.)*

I: *(Role-play a third situation from A or **B if time allows**.)*

I: *Thank you.*

No.2 Speaking Tests ESOL

Part 3 (3 minutes)

I: Now, Part Three. We're going to discuss something together.

We're planning to go to a music festival. Let's talk about what bands to see together and when and make some decisions. Here are some ideas. *(Hand over candidate's task sheet.)* I have some different ideas.

Take twenty seconds to think about what you want to say. (*20 seconds*.) Please start.

Interlocutor's Task Sheet

Bands I want to see:

- The Birds
- Jesse's Band
- Starving Artists
- Starry Eyes
- Love and Hate

Music-Festival Schedule:

- **10 am:** The Birds, The Flying Saucers, Tantrik Tunes
- **11 am:** Jesse's Band, The Hulks
- **noon:** Starving Artists
- **1 pm:** Jack's Pack, Starry Eyes, Life's Joke
- **2 pm:** Love and Hate, The Hornet's Nest

Candidate's Task Sheet

Bands I want to see:
- Tantrik Tunes

- Jesse's Band

- Starving Artists

- Starry Eyes

- The Hornet's Nest

Music-Festival Schedule:
- **10 am:** The Birds, The Flying Saucers, Tantrik Tunes

- **11 am:** Jesse's Band, The Hulks

- **noon:** Starving Artists

- **1 pm:** Jack's Pack, Starry Eyes, Life's Joke

- **2 pm:** Love and Hate, The Hornet's Nest

I: Thank you. *(Retrieve candidate's task sheet)*.

No.2 Speaking Tests ESOL

Part 4 (4 minutes including follow-up questions)

I: In Part Four you are going to talk on your own for about two minutes. Your topic is *(choose topic for candidate)*.

Topics
A **What can be done to stay healthy.**
B **Your favourite place to go on holiday.**
C **How to help keep your town clean.**

I: You now have thirty seconds to write some notes to help you. *(Hand over a piece of paper and pen/pencil.)* **So your topic is** *(repeat topic)*. *(Withdraw eye contact for thirty seconds. Leave recorder running.)*

I: *(Candidate's name)*, **please start.**

C: *(Talks.)*

I: *(When candidate has talked for a maximum of two minutes, say, 'Thank you', and then ask some follow-up questions.)*

Follow-up questions

What can be done to stay healthy

- What things do you do to keep healthy?
- How often should one see the doctor?
- What kind of diet is the healthiest?
- Is exercise important in order to stay healthy?

Your favourite place to go on holiday

- Where is this place?
- Why is it your favourite?
- What things are to do there?
- How often do you visit this place?

How to help keep your town clean

- What do you do to keep your town clean?
- What original ideas do you have to keep your town clean?
- In what ways does your community encourage people to keep the town clean?
- What do you know about recycling?

C: *(Responds.)*

I: Thank you, *(give candidate's name.)* **That is the end of the exam.**

Test 3

Part 1 (3 minutes)

I: International Spoken ESOL Exam, Communicator Level, *(give today's date)*. *(Give candidate's name.)* Exam begins.

Hello. My name's *(give full name)*. Can you spell your family name for me please?

C: *(Spells family name)*

I: Thank you. Which country are you from?

C: *(Responds)*

I: Thank you. Now, Part One. I'm going to ask you some questions about yourself and your ideas.

(Choose up to five questions, one from each of the different topic areas, as time allows. Name the topic; eg 'Now, Interests.')

Topics

Interests
- What is your favourite movie?
- Do you like adventurous holidays?
- Do you like computer games?
- What is your favourite kind of music?
- Would you be interested in taking part in any volunteer projects?

Your Home
- Where do you live?
- What kind of home do you live in?
- Who do you live with?
- What is your favourite thing about your home?

Your Family
- How many cousins do you have? Do you see them often?
- When was the last time you went to a big family event?
- Name some things that might make you start a fight with your brother/sister or with your parents.
- At what age do you think you will start your own family?

C: *(Responds.)*

I: *(Interlocutor makes brief responses and/or comments.)*

I: Thank you.

No.2 Speaking Tests ESOL

Part 2 (3 minutes)

I: Now, Part Two. We are going to role-play some situations. I want you to start or respond. First situation (*choose one situation from A*).

A

- We're colleagues. I start.
  May I use your printer? Mine doesn't work.

- I'm your car mechanic. I start.
  You're going to need new brakes.

- I'm your teacher. I start.
  Did you finish the assignment that was due today?

- We're friends. I start.
  Can I borrow some money from you?

C: *(Responds.)*
I: *(Role-play the situation with candidate - approximately two turns each.)*
I: *Second situation. (choose one situation from B).*

B

- We're friends. You've lost something you borrowed from me. You start.

- I'm your dentist. Your tooth hurts. You start.

- I work at a bank. You want to open a new account. You start.

- I'm an old friend. We haven't seen each other in years. You start.

C: *(Initiates.)*

I: *(Role-play the situation with candidate - approximately two turns each.)*

I: *(Role-play a third situation from **A** or **B** if time allows.)*

I: Thank you.

No.2 Speaking Tests ESOL

Part 3 (3 minutes)

I: Now, Part Three. We're going to discuss something together.

We're planning a party for a friend. Let's talk about what kind of party to have and make some decisions. Here are some ideas. *(Hand over candidate's task sheet.)* I have some different ideas.

Take twenty seconds to think about what you want to say. (*20 seconds*.) Please start.

Interlocutor's Task Sheet

Jesse's Party

Place: Jim's house or tina's house

Food: Only snacks

Type of Party: Costume party

Music: Jesse's favourite CDs

Time: Start at 6

LanguageCert Communicator CEFR Level B2 ESOL/SELT 朗思全真模拟题 1

Candidate's Task Sheet

Jesse's Party

Place: Recreation Centre

Food: Buffet

Type of Party: Surprise party

Music: Band

Time: Start at 10

I: Thank you. *(Retrieve candidate's task sheet).*

No.2 Speaking Tests ESOL

Part 4 (4 minutes including follow-up questions)

I: In Part Four you are going to talk on your own for about two minutes. Your topic is *(choose topic for candidate).*

Topics
A Fun places to go on holiday.
B Why family is important.
C Things to do on a day off.

I: You now have thirty seconds to write some notes to help you. *(Hand over piece of paper and pen/pencil.)* So your topic is *(repeat topic).* *(Withdraw eye contact for thirty seconds. Leave recorder running.)*

I: *(Candidate's name)*, please start.
C: *(Talks.)*
I: *(When candidate has talked for a maximum of two minutes, say, 'Thank you', and then ask some follow-up questions.)*

Follow-up questions

Fun places to go on holiday
○ What are some fun places to go on holiday?
○ Why would you choose to go to these places?
○ How many of these places have you been to?
○ What makes a place fun to go to on holiday?

Why family is important
○ What are some of the reasons that make you feel family is important?
○ What are some ways family members help each other?
○ What have you done to help your family recently?
○ How do you define "family"?

Things to do on a day off
- What do you do when you have a free day?
- How often do you have free days?
- What do most people your age do on their days off?
- What did you do the last time you had a day off?

C: *(Responds.)*

I: Thank you, *(give candidate's name.)* That is the end of the exam.

No.2 Speaking Tests ESOL

Test 4

Part 1 (3 minutes)

I: International Spoken ESOL Exam, Communicator Level, *(give today's date)*. *(Give candidate's name.)* Exam begins.

Hello. My name's *(give full name)*. Can you spell your family name for me please?

C: *(Spells family name)*

I: Thank you. Which country are you from?

C: *(Responds)*

I: Thank you. Now, Part One. I'm going to ask you some questions about yourself and your ideas.

(Choose up to five questions, one from each of the different topic areas, as time allows. Name the topic; eg 'Now, Your Home.')

Topics

Your Home
- Where do you live?
- Are you satisfied with the area that you live in?
- How do you feel about moving to another house/area/town?
- What is more important to you: having shops, and facilities nearby, or living in a quiet and relaxing place?

Jobs
- What job would you like to do if you had the choice?
- Are you a person who cares more about having a career or having a family?
- "*We work to live*" or "*We live to work*", what is your view?
- How can you achieve job satisfaction? By working in a job you enjoy or by working in a job that pays a lot of money?

Interests

- What music do you enjoy listening to?
- Are you the type of person that gets information through the internet, the radio, television or newspapers? Explain the reason(s) for your choice.
- Do you have any hobbies? Which one(s)?
- What is your relationship with art?

The Environment

- What problems are there concerning the environment in the area that you live in?
- In your neighbourhood, is recycling a part of people's everyday life?
- Pollution is a very serious issue in our days. In what way(s) are you trying to protect the environment?
- Are you a member of any environmental group? Have you ever considered being one?

Activities and Sports

- Which sports do you enjoy playing or watching?
- What type of life do you lead? A healthy one or one that allows you to smoke, eat what you want, etc.?
- How do you feel about having a balanced lifestyle?
  Do you consider it to be a restriction or a benefit?
- What do you do when you feel stressed?

C: *(Responds.)*

I: *(Interlocutor makes brief responses and/or comments.)*

I: Thank you.

Part 2 (3 minutes)

I: Now, Part Two. We are going to role-play some situations. I want you to start or respond. First situation *(choose one situation from A)*.

A

- I'm your mum/dad. I start.

  I need your help with shopping.

- I'm your boss. I start.

  Congratulations! You've just got the promotion.
  You are going to work 12 hours per day.
  How do you feel about that?

- I'm your neighbour. I start.

  Hi, you haven't seen my dog, have you? I can't find him anywhere.

- I'm a stranger. I start.

  Excuse me. Is there a nice place to have lunch near here?

C: *(Responds.)*
I: *(Role-play the situation with candidate - approximately two turns each.)*
I: *Second situation. (choose one situation from B).*

B

- I'm your husband/wife. I need you to pack my luggage as I'm flying in two hours. You start.

- We're roommates. You broke my favourite vase. You start.

- I'm your boss. You want to leave work early to go to the dentist. You start.

- I'm a police officer. You are lost in a strange city and you need directions to the train station. You start.

C   (Initiates.)

I: (Role-play the situation with candidate - approximately two turns each.)

I: (Role-play a third situation from **A** or **B if time allows**.)

I: Thank you.

Part 3 (3 minutes)

I: Now, Part Three. We're going to discuss something together.
We're planning a day out with some friends. Let's talk about what things we could do and make some decisions. Here are some ideas. *(Hand over candidate's task sheet.)* I have some different ideas.

Interlocutor's Task Sheet

A day out

- swimming pool - £5 admission

- cinema - romantic film showing - £6.50 per ticket

- go for pizza

- go to a museum or gallery - free entry

Candidate's Task Sheet

A day out

- go to beach - free

- take a picnic

- go to a nightclub - £8 to get in

- go to a theme park - £10 admission

I: Thank you. *(Retrieve candidate's task sheet)*.

No.2 Speaking Tests ESOL

Part 4 (4 minutes including follow-up questions)

I: In Part Four you are going to talk on your own for about two minutes. Your topic is *(choose topic for candidate)*.

Topics
A   A person who is very important to you.
B   Pros and Cons of your country's educational system.
C   Marriage in your country.

I: You now have thirty seconds to write some notes to help you. *(Hand over a piece of paper and pen/pencil.)* So your topic is *(repeat topic). (Withdraw eye contact for thirty seconds. Leave recorder running.)*

I: *(Candidate's name)*, please start.

C: *(Talks.)*

I: *(When candidate has talked for a maximum of two minutes, say, 'Thank you', and then ask some follow-up questions.)*

Follow–up questions

A person who is very important to you
- What qualities do you admire in a person?
- Who do you tend to talk to if you have a problem and why?
- What would you like to change about yourself if you could and why?
- "Show me your friends and I'll tell you who you are", what's your opinion?

Pros and Cons of your country's educational system
- Do you consider work to be something time-consuming or a necessity for your well-being?
- Do you think that your country's educational system is fair for everybody, poor or rich?

- Would you study something for practical reasons or just because you like it?
- Studying in a university or a technical school?

Marriage in your country
- Which types of family exist and which one do you consider the most balanced for a child's upbringing (nuclear family, single parent family, etc.)?
- Do you believe that throughout your life only one person will complete you? Or is it just a romantic way of viewing love?
- Are you making plans for the future or are you more spontaneous in what life brings?
- What is the best age for someone to get married?

C: *(Responds.)*

I: Thank you, *(give candidate's name.)* **That is the end of the exam.**

Test 5

Part 1 (3 minutes)

I: International Spoken ESOL Exam, Communicator Level, *(give today's date)*. *(Give candidate's name.)* Exam begins.

Hello. My name's *(give full name)*. Can you spell your family name for me please?

C: *(Spells family name)*

I: Thank you. Which country are you from?

C: *(Responds)*

I: Thank you. Now, Part One. I'm going to ask you some questions about yourself and your ideas.

(Choose up to five questions, one from each of the different topic areas, as time allows. Name the topic; eg 'Now, Your Family.')

Topics

Your Family
- Can you tell me something about your family?
- Do you have any brothers and/or sisters?
  Do you get along with them?
- Do you consider yourself a cooperative person or not?
- Do you help with housework and daily chores?

Leisure Time
- What do you like to do in your free time?
- Are you an active individual? In what ways?
- Creativity in life is very important. In what ways do you usually express yourself?
- Is there enough free time for you to refill your energy for your routine days?

Lifestyle

- What food do you like? Are you a vegetarian or a meat eater?
- Are you practising any sport? Any connection between your diet and a sport philosophy (i.e. yoga)?
- Smoking is a dangerous habit, though many people smoke without considering the hazards to their health.
  Why do you feel this happens? Can you suggest some possible solutions?
- Would you ever consider cultivating your own products in order to eat healthy food?

Holidays

- Where did you go on your last holiday? Did you enjoy it?
- Any plans for this summer?
- Do you prefer going on holiday with your parents/friends or with your wife/husband/boyfriend/girlfriend?
- Holidays are a way to relax and focus on yourself. But is a week or two enough to do that?

Art

- Tell me about a film that you enjoyed.
- Describe the type of person you are when it comes to art.
- If you had a talent, would you try to achieve something with it or would you prefer to have a regular job?
- Have you ever felt that something you've read in a book, listened to, seen in a play, has made you a better person or helped you in any way?

C: *(Responds.)*

I: *(Interlocutor makes brief responses and / or comments.)*

I: Thank you.

No.2 Speaking Tests ESOL

Part 2 (3 minutes)

I: Now, Part Two. We are going to role-play some situations. I want you to start or respond. First situation *(choose one situation from A).*

A

- I'm your friend. I start.

  Hi, I'm having a party next week. I'd like you to come; do you think it would be a good idea to make it a barbecue party?

- I'm a stranger. I start.

  Excuse me. Where would you recommend I go for a coffee around here?

- I'm a tourist. I start.

  Could you direct me to the post office?

- I'm a taxi driver. I start.

  Sorry madam, I can't give you a lift; I have just finished working.

C: *(Responds.)*
I: *(Role-play the situation with candidate - approximately two turns each.)*
I: *Second situation. (choose one situation from **B**).*

B

- I'm a colleague of yours. You need some help to finish a project. You start.

- I'm a waiter. You want to complain because your food is cold. You start.

- I'm a police officer. You need to get a new identity card. You start.

- I'm a librarian. You have to do a project and need more than two books the library can lend you. You start.

C: *(Initiates.)*

I: *(Role-play the situation with candidate - approximately two turns each.)*

I: *(Role-play a third situation from A or **B if time allows**.)*

I: Thank you.

Part 3 (3 minutes)

I: Now, Part Three. We're going to discuss something together.

We're planning a weekend away. Let's talk about where we could go and make some decisions. Here are some ideas. *(Hand over candidate's task sheet.)* I have some different ideas.

Take twenty seconds to think about what you want to say. *(20 seconds.)* Please start.

Interlocutor's Task Sheet

Weekend away

- theme-park for the weekend

- walking holiday in the country

- city break - go to another big city

- go to an exhibition

Candidate's Task Sheet

Weekend away

- Greek island - stay in hotel

- campsite in the forest

- mountain skiing

- going to the theatre, followed by expensive dinner

I: Thank you. *(Retrieve candidate's task sheet).*

Part 4 (4 minutes including follow-up questions)

I: In Part Four you are going to talk on your own for about two minutes. Your topic is *(choose topic for candidate).*

Topics
A **A day that you will never forget.**
B **The hazards of technology.**
C **Beauty issues.**

I: You now have thirty seconds to write some notes to help you. *(Hand over a piece of paper and pen/pencil.)* So your topic is *(repeat topic). (Withdraw eye contact for thirty seconds. Leave recorder running.)*

I: *(Candidate's name),* **please start.**

C: *(Talks.)*

I: *(When candidate has talked for a maximum of two minutes, say, 'Thank you', and then ask some follow-up questions.)*

Follow-up questions
A day that you will never forget
- What was your most unforgettable day?
- Why did you choose that day?
- What was the happiest moment in your life?
- What inspires you and motivates you in life?

The hazards of technology
- Give the pros and cons of using Internet in everyday life.
- Is it a good thing or a bad thing when machines can do a job better than people?
- Why do people have so much stress in their lives? Is it connected to consumerism?
- Mobile phones are a part of our everyday life, but what are the negative aspects of them?

Beauty issues
- Why do people like stories where someone ugly becomes beautiful?
- Racism has many forms. Have you ever had to face something like that?
- Do you use any beauty products?
- Do you think it is OK to test beauty products on animals?

C: (Responds.)

I: Thank you, *(give candidate's name.)* That is the end of the exam.

No.3

Audio Scripts

LanguageCert Communicator CEFR Level B2 ESOL/SELT 朗思全真模拟题 1

Test 1

Part one, part one.

You will hear some short conversations. You will hear each conversation twice. Choose the correct answer for each conversation. *(15 seconds.)*

Number one. Number one. *(6 seconds)*

M: I'm going for a quick shower.

W: Wait a minute, I'm not sure you have time!

M: When do we need to leave?

(Wait 10 seconds before repeating.)

(10 seconds)

Number two. Number two. *(6 seconds)*

W: Oh, there you are! I've been looking for you.

M: What's the matter? I'll see you tonight, right?

W: I doubt I can come to your party.

(Wait 10 seconds before repeating.)

(10 seconds)

Number three. Number three. *(6 seconds)*

M: Why the long face?

W: It just seems so hard to meet new people.

M: Cheer up, I can introduce you to my friend Brian sometime.

(Wait 10 seconds before repeating.)

(10 seconds)

Number four. Number four. *(6 seconds)*

W: Mary seems a bit on edge.

M: She says she's going to quit her job.

W: Really? Is she serious?

(Wait 10 seconds before repeating.)

(10 seconds)

Number five. Number five. *(6 seconds)*

M: You're soaked!

W: I can't believe this rain - the wind is blowing it sideways! The drops were hitting me like bullets!

M: I haven't seen weather like this in years.

(Wait 10 seconds before repeating.)

(10 seconds)

Number six. Number six. *(6 seconds)*

M: There's so little going on in this town.

W: There's always something happening at the community centre, though.

M: Are you going to the concert there, tomorrow night?

(Wait 10 seconds before repeating.)

(10 seconds)

Number seven. Number seven. *(6 seconds)*

W: Mr. Smith? Didn't you say you'd promote our performance?

M: Of course! Is there a problem?

W: It's just that there aren't many people here today.

(Wait 10 seconds before repeating.)

(10 seconds)

That is the end of Part One.

Part two, part two.

You will hear some conversations. You will hear each conversation twice. Choose the correct answers for each conversation. *(10 seconds.)*

Conversation 1

W: Oh my! Hello! I haven't seen you in ages. What are you doing here?

M: Well, I was actually just driving through and I remembered that you live here now. I called up your old roommate and she had your address so I decided to stop by to surprise you.

W: What a lovely surprise! Please come in and have a cup of coffee. I don't think we've seen each other since we graduated from university. In fact, I don't even remember the last time we spoke!

M: Yes, I know. It has been quite a while, hasn't it? I've thought about you a lot over the years though. It is sad that we lost touch. Are you married?

W: No, I'm not. I'm actually back in school. I decided to go back for my Master's in Education. That's why I moved here.

M: Incredible. I'm very impressed. I finished Law school a few years ago and since then I've been very busy with work, but I'm thinking about taking some time off this summer. Do you have plans? Maybe we could do some travelling together.

W: That's a wonderful idea.

(Wait 10 seconds before repeating.) (10 seconds)
Now, look at the questions for Conversation Two. (10 seconds)

Conversation 2

M: Are you looking for any particular style?

W: Well, no, but, I mean... OK, my bedroom is off-white and the door is made of a light-coloured wood so I need the furniture to match with that, but otherwise I haven't really decided what I want. I thought you could help me.

M: Well I certainly can, but you're going to have to make some decisions. Do you want a white bedroom set or a wood-coloured one? We could have your furniture match your door if you wanted.

W: No, I don't think that's a good idea. Actually, I was thinking maybe I should paint the room a very light blue and then get all white furniture. Maybe I could even paint the door. My husband loves blue. What do you think? Would he like a blue bedroom? Or maybe a subtle pink?

M: Ma'am I am here to help you buy furniture, I'm not a designer!

No.3 Audio Scripts

(Wait 10 seconds before repeating.) (10 seconds)

Now, look at the questions for Conversation Three. (10 seconds)

Conversation 3

W: I've worked in retail for the past 5 years, at R. C Penny's on the East coast but I've just moved out here, which is why I'm applying for this job.

M: Sounds good. What was your job description at Penny's?

W: Well, basically I was just a salesgirl. I helped people find outfits and worked on the register. But I was really good at what I did and won "salesperson of the month" six times!

M: You are aware that the position you're applying for, here, is not a salesperson position?

W: Well, yes, sales manager, right? That's basically the same thing, isn't it, just being a salesperson while managing other people?

M: Not at all, Miss. Sales manager means you'll be behind the scenes not really interacting with customers but rather seeing that everything runs smoothly.

W: Oh. Uh well...

M: We do have some salesperson positions open. Do you want to reapply for one of those?

W: Oh yes, I would.

(Wait 10 seconds before repeating.) (10 seconds)

That is the end of Part Two.

Part three, part three.

You will hear someone talking. You will hear the person twice. Complete the information. Write short answers of one to five words. *(1 minute.)*

[beep]

Hello counsellors, and thanks for getting here so early. I want to go over this week's schedule for camp. That's for the dates of July 1st to the 7th. We'll worry about next week's schedule, because it will be different, and I don't want to confuse anyone. Alright, please take down notes, so you'll remember everything tomorrow when the kids arrive and start asking questions.

So, tomorrow, Monday, we'll have a football tournament going on all day and then at night we'll have a little awards ceremony to congratulate the winning team. This will help everyone to get to know each other. For any children who really dislike football, or have injuries or health issues, there will be an arts and crafts table by the dining hall, but I want you to do everything you can, within reason, to get all the children to join in the football tournament.

From Tuesday to Thursday, we're planning a lot of water-related activities including swimming and boating. It's supposed to be very hot, so the kids will really enjoy being in the water. Just a safety note, here; remember that I want at least two of you counsellors present at the lake at all times while the children are doing water activities. This is absolutely critical - no exceptions! I don't mind how the four of you split up the duties, but make sure to look out for each other and see that everyone gets food and toilet breaks when needed. So, this means that you won't all go to lunch together, right? You'll go in groups of two. I'm sorry if it sounds obvious, but last year the counsellors seemed to think that the two on duty rule didn't apply to lunch time!

Right! What else? We'll have a barbecue on the lakeshore Thursday evening, so you'll need to inform me by Thursday if any of the children in your cabin are vegetarians or have other special dietary needs. There will also be a chance for the kids to take a day-cruise on Thursday, but it costs an extra ten pounds.

On Friday we'll have an arts and crafts day, with tables set up on the sports field so that the children take turns visiting. Your main duties here will be 'traffic control'; you know, make sure everyone gets to have a go at candle making and the whole camp doesn't descend on the watercolour table at the same time - that sort of thing. There'll be a very special surprise on Friday evening - an outdoor film "Casablanca" will be shown on the sports field at 7 pm after everyone's finished dinner.

On the weekend, we'll be taking a trip to Fish Lake to go camping. We'll leave at 6 am on Saturday and we'll return on Sunday evening.

I'll be here for the rest of the morning if anyone has any questions.

(Wait 10 seconds before repeating.) (10 seconds)

You will now have two minutes to read through and check your answers. *(2 minutes)*

[beep]

That is the end of Part Three.

Part four, part four.

You will hear a conversation. You will hear the conversation twice. Choose the correct answers. *(20 seconds)*

M: I have to say, your sister really did give us an amazing present. Two tickets to New York City! We have to start planning the trip, we leave in three weeks and we have only the plane tickets. We haven't even booked hotels or figured out what we want to see there.

W: I can still barely believe we're really going! Jenny is the best sister ever. This is going to be amazing and romantic and just tons of fun. Let's start at the beginning. What do we want to do in NYC?

M: Well, I definitely want to see the Statue of Liberty. And of course the Empire State Building. I think we should just get a central hotel and stay there the whole time.

W: Oh, I can't wait to go to museums there! I'm also dying to go shopping. I need some beautiful New York shoes.

M: The last thing you need is another pair of shoes. So what about a hotel? Somewhere central? According to my guidebook the Centre City Heights Hotel looks good ... it seems to be in the centre of everything and if you book for a week you save $200. It also comes with free breakfast.

W: Are you sure we should stay in the same hotel for the whole week? Maybe we should try some different places.

M: That's going to make things much more difficult, let's just stick with one place. Look, it even has a swimming pool!

W: How much is it? More than $200 a night?

M: It is $250 a night ... so multiply that by six nights ... $1,500 ... minus the $200 discount ... $1,300. That sounds fine, we deserve it!

W: What about day trips? Is there anything we want to do outside the city?

M: Actually, yes. Do you remember my cousin Benjamin? He lives on Long Island about 3 hours away from the city but right on the water. I thought maybe we could visit him for a day.

W: That sounds good. I wonder if there is good shopping on Long Island.

M: Have you decided what museums you want to visit?

W: Well definitely the Metropolitan Museum of Art. The 19th century European paintings are supposed to be absolutely amazing! I was also going to say we should go to the new September 11th Ground Zero Museum but I think it would be too depressing. I hate sad things like that. I would like to visit the Museum of Natural History and the New York Fashion Museum as well.

M: I am not going with you to a fashion museum. Isn't shopping enough? Why would anyone need a shopping museum?

W: I knew you'd say that.

(Wait 10 seconds before repeating.) (10 seconds)

That is the end of Part Four.

You now have two hours and ten minutes to complete the rest of the paper.

No.3 Audio Scripts

Test 2

Part one, part one.
You will hear some short conversations. You will hear each conversation twice. Choose the correct answer for each conversation. *(15 seconds.)*

Number one. Number one. *(6 seconds)*

M: you're going to the library now? I thought we could go out for some food.

W: I'm really so busy this afternoon.

M: What are you doing later?

(Wait 10 seconds before repeating.)

(10 seconds)

Number two. Number two. *(6 seconds)*

W: Your first exhibition of paintings! You must be so excited!

M: I'm more nervous than excited, actually.

W: Are there going to be many people there?

(Wait 10 seconds before repeating.)

(10 seconds)

Number three. Number three. *(6 seconds)*

M: I'm afraid I don't understand.

W: Uh, okay. Well...

M: Would you mind writing the address down for me?

(Wait 10 seconds before repeating.)

(10 seconds)

Number four. Number four. *(6 seconds)*

W: We should all go sit in the accountant's sunny south-facing office.

M: Look at you in your hat and scarf !

159

W: It's so cold in here!

(Wait 10 seconds before repeating.)

(10 seconds)

Number five. Number five. *(6 seconds)*

M: Have you checked the weather forecast?

W: No, why?

M: I hear it's going to rain all next week.

(Wait 10 seconds before repeating.)

(10 seconds)

Number six. Number six. *(6 seconds)*

W: You know, they're planning a protest at Park Square tomorrow.

M: My bank's in Park Square.

W: You aren't going tomorrow, are you?

(Wait 10 seconds before repeating.)

(10 seconds)

Number seven. Number seven. *(6 seconds)*

W: Gloria's asked me ten times today to take her along.

M: See, you just upset her by telling her.

W: I don't see why I can't bring my little sister with us.

(Wait 10 seconds before repeating.)

(10 seconds)

That is the end of Part One.

Part two, part two.

You will hear some conversations. You will hear each conversation twice. Choose the correct answers for each conversation. *(10 seconds.)*

Conversation 1

W: Good morning! May I help you?

M: I need a gift for my girlfriend. It is our one-year anniversary. I really have no idea what to get her, so I thought I'd try a big store like this one instead of a specialised boutique.

W: Well you've come to the right place. How much money were you thinking of spending?

M: Umm... I don't know... 20 pounds?

W: You know, these days 20 pounds doesn't go so far. If you extended your budget a bit it would be easier to find the perfect gift.

M: Well, okay, you seem to know what you're talking about.

W: How about perfume? What does your girlfriend wear?

M: Umm... It is kind of fruity smelling. Like... apples?

W: Maybe we should try handbags. Does she have a favourite designer?

M: No, I don't think so. There's a brown bag she has that she likes a lot.

W: I know! Jewelry. Look at this beautiful white gold bracelet. It is only 100 pounds on sale.

M: That's way more than I wanted to pay though. I was thinking... shampoo... or something. Maybe I should just take her to a nice restaurant.

W: Do you want to stay with this girl for another year? Trust me, get the bracelet.

M: Okay, you win. I'll take it.

(Wait 10 seconds before repeating.) (10 seconds)
Now, look at the questions for Conversation Two. (10 seconds)

Conversation 2

M: I'm going to be your personal instructor today so if you have any questions or concerns before we begin please let me know.

W: As for questions, I don't know where to begin... and concerns... well, I'm a little nervous right now.

M: Don't be! You'll be fine. I promise we'll take it easy. Now let's start at the beginning. Are your skis securely on? Are you warm enough?

W: I'm hot under all these layers and yes, my skis are on. Let's go already.

M: First, some instructions. Be careful on the lift, the chair will come from behind but all you have to do is sit at the right time. When we get to the top of the mountain we'll lift the bar and get off the chair. I want you to put the front of your skis together, making a pie slice shape, and slowly guide down off the lift until you stop. It's easy!

(Wait 10 seconds before repeating.) (10 seconds)
Now, look at the questions for Conversation Three. (10 seconds)

Conversation 3

W: How are you doing? Are the kids doing well?

M: Yeah, they are, but things are a little crazy at home right now. Cindy has been working overtime every night so I've been really busy taking care of the kids.

W: Do you not usually take care of the kids...?

M: Well, I do, but to be honest Cindy takes care of most of it usually. I get exhausted! I can't work a full day and then come home to drive the kids to practice and make dinner... it's exhausting.

W: But Cindy works full time, too. And for that matter, I work full time and come home and do all that. You need to start helping out more at home, Ben.

M: Yeah, I guess I do, but it just isn't what I'm good at. I like playing with the kids and I mow the lawn and stuff... but I just wouldn't be able to clean the house or make an edible meal. That's just how it works.

W: If we weren't old friends I don't think I'd like you very much. Relationships should be equal. You need to pull your own weight.

M: It just depends on the relationship.

(Wait 10 seconds before repeating.) (10 seconds)
That is the end of Part Two.

Part three, part three.

You will hear someone talking. You will hear the person twice. Complete the information. Write short answers of one to five words. *(1 minute.)*

[beep]

Good morning team! I'm going to go over the schedule for today's football clinic. First, we're all going to go for a slow 3-mile run to warm up. Then we're going to split into 3 groups which will each work on a different skill. We'll switch groups every 30 minutes.

Group A will work on defence, both jockeying and tackles. Remember, you don't always need to tackle an opponent to slow their progress. Jockeying denies your opponent time and space, and it's a good tactic to allow your team-mates to get back in position. Though, of course, you also need to be able to tackle. If your team is not in possession of the ball it's obviously crucial to get it back. There are many different ways to achieve this, but the block tackle is the best and most common method. When properly timed, the sliding tackle is a very effective skill, and it also looks good, but remember this is a last-ditch tackle. The problem is that it leaves the defender lying on the ground and so temporarily out of the game. And if you get the timing wrong you'll give away a foul.

Group B will work on passing. Passing quickly gets the ball up field and reduces the risks of giving away possession. The inside of the foot provides the greatest accuracy for passing. But it is difficult to generate power and it is also easy for an opponent to see where you are intending to pass the ball. For those reasons, it is best to use this skill just for short passes. We will focus on other options, today, for long passes.

Group C will work on ball control. You always hear how important getting the ball under control is, so, alongside passing, this is an area that will hugely improve your game if you can get it right. The basics of control are the same whether you are controlling the ball with your feet, thigh, chest or head. We'll cover all the basics.

After this, we'll stop for lunch. A lunch in the cafeteria costs 4 pounds, or you can go to any of the restaurants around the corner. Your lunch break will be for an hour and a half, so please keep track of the time and be back at 1:30 promptly.

After lunch, there's an optional film called "Football Stars". It lasts 15 minutes and will be shown in the gymnasium. It's an inspiring film, and quite enjoyable, so I'd encourage all of you to see it. But if you don't choose to go, please do some ball skills practice out front.

After this, we will have video training for the rest of the afternoon. The clinic ends at 5 pm. Now let's go have some fun!

(Wait 10 seconds before repeating.) (10 seconds)

You will now have two minutes to read through and check your answers. *(2 minutes)*
[beep]
That is the end of Part Three.

Part four, part four.

You will hear a conversation. You will hear the conversation twice. Choose the correct answers. *(20 seconds.)*

W: I am so excited Aaron! We're moving in together, finally!

M: This is a big day. I hope it doesn't get too hot. I hate moving boxes when it is hot out.

W: I can't wait to start unpacking. Where should we put the couch? Under the window?

M: I don't know; we'll have to see. Where are the guys with the truck? Shouldn't they be here by now?

W: They're coming at 9:30. We have all day, don't worry. Did you pick up the keys yet?

M: No, I thought you did. I guess we'll have to stop by the estate agents' office before we go. Maybe I should leave early and do that.

W: It doesn't matter; we both have to sign our lease before we start moving in anyway. It isn't even official yet.

M: It might as well be. Are you sure you want this old white couch? We could easily buy a new one.

W: I love that couch. It is the most comfortable couch I've ever sat on. We can't get rid of it.

M: How much are we paying each month? 600 pounds plus utilities?

W: No! 650. Did you ever READ the lease?

M: I just forgot. 50 pounds doesn't make much of a difference anyway. This place is a fortune though. I'm paying a lot less than that for the place I'm in now. Only 400 pounds a month.

W: But it is just you there now... this will be OUR place, of course it is going to be more expensive. Remember when you lived with Tim and Brad? Rent was something like 1,000 pounds a month but it was split between you three.

M: Yeah. I guess you're right. We're going to have to buy some new furniture soon. My stuff and your stuff don't go well together.

W: What's that supposed to mean? Do you expect me to get rid of my things?

M: I didn't say that, I just mean we're going to have to make some decisions about what to keep and what new things we want. I like things to look put-together. Understand?

W: I guess. What time do we need to be at the estate agents' by? 12:00? Or 12:30?

M: I think if we're there by 1 we'll be fine. Don't get so anxious it is only 9:15.

(Wait 10 seconds before repeating.) (10 seconds)

That is the end of Part Four.

You now have two hours and ten minutes to complete the rest of the paper.

Test 3

Part one, part one.

You will hear some short conversations. You will hear each conversation twice. Choose the correct answer for each conversation. *(15 seconds.)*

Number one. Number one. *(6 seconds)*

W: Your exams finished, so, I guess you'll be home for Aunty Bella's party?

M: I haven't got a flight yet, Mum. I'm not sure.

W: When are you coming?

(Wait 10 seconds before repeating.)

(10 seconds)

Number two. Number two. *(6 seconds)*

M: Have you written down the appointment?

W: Yes; Wednesday afternoon, 4pm.

M: Alright. And it's Wednesday the 24th, correct?

(Wait 10 seconds before repeating.)

(10 seconds)

Number three. Number three. *(6 seconds)*

W: Do you think we'll get to the airport in time if we take the bus?

M: Yes, there's plenty of time.

W: Are you sure?

(Wait 10 seconds before repeating.)

(10 seconds)

Number four. Number four. *(6 seconds)*

M: Alright, let's get started.

W: Shouldn't we wait until everyone's present before we begin the meeting?

M: Oh, where's Tom? I thought he was here.

(Wait 10 seconds before repeating.)

(10 seconds)

Number five. Number five. *(6 seconds)*

W: What a lovely summer we're having!

M: Well, it's nice for us, but not for the plants and trees!

W: Don't worry, I hear it rained up north yesterday.

(Wait 10 seconds before repeating.)

(10 seconds)

Number six. Number six. *(6 seconds)*

M: Are you going to the opera on Friday?

W: I don't know; I haven't decided.

M: Do you think the tickets will be expensive?

(Wait 10 seconds before repeating.)

(10 seconds)

Number seven. Number seven. *(6 seconds)*

W: How do I set up this antivirus programme?

M: First you need to go onto their website and find the download button.

(Wait 10 seconds before repeating.)

(10 seconds)

That is the end of Part One.

Part two, part two.

You will hear some conversations. You will hear each conversation twice. Choose the correct answers for each conversation *(10 seconds)*

Conversation 1

W: Do you have this shirt in a smaller size?

M: No, we don't. But that one might fit you, this brand runs rather small.

W: What are you saying? It looks huge!

M: How about that same shirt in pink, then?

W: I hate pink. Do you have it in green?

M: Yes, we do, but not in the size you want.

W: This is the problem with small boutiques. You don't ever have what I need. I'm going to start shopping in department stores. Or maybe I'll just shop from home online.

M: Don't be discouraged. There are lots of other shirts here, and buying from a small store not only means you are supporting a small community business, but when you buy more original clothing fewer people will be walking about with the same thing on. You'll be original and stylish.

W: Those are good points. Do you have anything in my size, not pink and original?

M: Well, we have this beautiful dress here. No one has bought one like it yet, so you'd be the only one in town with it.

W: It is gorgeous! I'll take it. I guess small shops aren't so bad after all!

(Wait 10 seconds before repeating.) (10 seconds)
Now, look at the questions for Conversation Two. (10 seconds)

Conversation 2

M: How about we just take the kids up to my mother's place for the week? There's that lake nearby, and she'd love to see them.

W: I don't want to go there again. Every year we plan on some big exciting trip and end up going to your mother's.

M: Well, what do you suggest, dear?

W: Let's go camping. It would be good for the kids to get some fresh air and we have all that camping gear that we haven't used.

M: That's true. Do you think they'd like that?

W: They'd prefer to go to an amusement park or to a tropical resort, but we can't afford that.

M: Very true. Okay, let's go check out our camping gear!

(Wait 10 seconds before repeating.) (10 seconds)

Now, look at the questions for Conversation Three. (10 seconds)

Conversation 3

W: Have you heard from Earl lately?

M: Not since he moved to Briarsville. What about you?

W: Nope. It seems that when people move that's always the last we hear from them. Our little community seems to be shrinking pretty fast!

M: Well, my family sure isn't planning a move. Beth and I are so happy here and the kids have finally settled down at school. How are you and Tom and the kids doing?

W: Quite well. Tom just got a promotion and the kids seem really happy. I really do love this town. I'm glad we moved here and I'm glad we met such great neighbours like you and Beth!

M: Ah, thanks. We're glad we met you too. This is a great little town, really. We hope to be here forever and we hope to be great neighbours forever, too!

(Wait 10 seconds before repeating.)
(10 seconds)
That is the end of Part Two.

Part three, part three.

You will hear someone talking. You will hear the person twice. Complete the information. Write short answers of one to five words. *(1 minute.)*

[beep]

Good morning students of Brookfield School. It is field athletics day today! I know many of you have been looking forward to this for a long time, so I'll make this as short as possible so we can begin! First, I just want to mention the history of athletics. The original and only event at the first Olympics in 776 BC was a stadium-length foot race on a track. You could call this the first athletics event! In the Classical era the Panhellenic Games were held at several locations, every few years. Athletics was included in the first modern Olympic Games in 1896 and has formed their backbone ever since. Women were first allowed to participate in track and field events in the 1928 Olympics.

Alright, we will begin at 8 am, when there will be a chance for everyone to warm-up on the main field. Warm up activities are a crucial part of any sports training so I want to go over some warm-up techniques now, just to be sure everyone remembers them. Warm-up can be broken up into three parts; the general warm up, static stretching; and dynamic stretching. The general warm up should consist of about 20 minutes of a light physical activity, like walking, jogging, skipping or easy aerobics, anything to increase your heart rate. Static stretching is next, and you should aim to stretch all muscle groups, being sure to stretch the opposing muscle groups too. Static stretching should last for about ten minutes. We'll skip dynamic stretching since I know most of you aren't familiar with it, and it can be dangerous if done incorrectly.

After warming up, around 8:30, everyone must choose the sports events they want to take part in. You all must choose at least one of the offered events including (which include) the long jump, high jump, 100 and 800 metre races, and relay races. If you're really keen, you should have time to participate in training for all the events, though you must choose no more than three to compete in.

At 9 am we will begin the training for the competition. On Field A will be the high-jump and the long jump. On Track A we will have the 100 and 800 metre races. On Track B we will have the relay races. We will rotate events throughout the day. The competition will take place from approximately 12 to 1pm. After the competition you're free to go to the refreshment tables, relax, and talk amongst yourselves.

At 2 pm we will hold the awards ceremony on the main field. That's it everyone! Let's go and have a great day and good luck!

(Wait 10 seconds before repeating.) (10 seconds)
You will now have two minutes to read through and check your answers. *(2 minutes)*
[beep]
That is the end of Part Three.

Part four, part four.

You will hear a conversation. You will hear the conversation twice. Choose the correct answers. *(20 seconds.)*

M: In honour of your birthday, I think we should finally get a puppy. I know you've been wanting one for ages.

W: Really? I think that's an AMAZING idea! Can we go today? What kind of puppy? Do we have enough room in the house? This is SO exciting.

M: Slow down, slow down. I was thinking of a big dog, or a German Shepherd, or maybe even a Great Dane.

W: No, definitely not a big dog. I want a little dog; something I can pick up and cuddle.

M: Oh, come on, a small dog can't protect us.

W: I thought this was MY dog. I want something cute.

M: It will be OUR dog, I just thought your birthday would be a fun time to get it. Why don't we agree on a medium-sized dog?

W: Okay. Medium is okay. Big dogs scare me, though. When I was five I was at this little country store with my mother. They had cows at the back and while my mum talked to the store owner I sat on the back steps and watched the cows and ate a biscuit. Suddenly the dog of the store owner, a mean looking German Shepherd, lunged at me to try to get the biscuit. Unfortunately he also got my nose. I was rushed to the emergency room and you can still see the scar where he bit me.

M: I cannot believe! You've never told me that story before. It seems odd that you still love dogs so much after an experience like that.

W: I know. But as I said, I'm a little scared of big dogs still.

M: Medium-sized dog it is. Do you want a girl or a boy?

W: Definitely a girl.

M: Why? I hear male dogs are better behaved and training classes are cheaper.

W: Where did you hear that? That doesn't make any sense at all. I just want a cute little girl, that's all.

(Wait 10 seconds before repeating.) (10 seconds)

That is the end of Part Four.

You now have two hours and ten minutes to complete the rest of the paper.

Test 4

Part one, part one.
You will hear some short conversations. You will hear each conversation twice. Choose the correct answer for each conversation. *(15 seconds.)*

Number one. Number one. *(6 seconds)*

W: I think I'm the only one that does anything around here!

M: What are you talking about?

W: The least you could do is help me carry these shopping bags.

(Wait 10 seconds before repeating.)

(10 seconds)

Number two. Number two. *(6 seconds)*

M: I'm so bored.

W: Well, then make a change in your life!

M: You're right. Maybe I'll have my hair cut.

(Wait 10 seconds before repeating.)

(10 seconds)

Number three. Number three. *(6 seconds)*

M: Excuse me; where can I find platform 12?

W: Just there to your left, sir.

M: Do you know when the next train to London is?

(Wait 10 seconds before repeating.)

(10 seconds)

Number four. Number four. *(6 seconds)*

W: I'm so uncomfortable, I can't concentrate on my work!

M: Why? What's wrong?

W: I'm feeling rather cold.

(Wait 10 seconds before repeating.)

(10 seconds)

Number five. Number five. *(6 seconds)*

M: Really? You caught a shoplifter?

W: I noticed her because she was so little, no more than 6 years old.

M: And she was by herself?

(Wait 10 seconds before repeating.)

(10 seconds)

Number six. Number six. *(6 seconds)*

W: Have you taught before Mr. Milroy?

M: Yes, I taught at a secondary school last term.

W: And what did you gain from that experience?

(Wait 10 seconds before repeating.)

(10 seconds)

Number seven. Number seven. *(6 seconds)*

W: I've lost my keys!

M: Oh, no!

W: Can you help me to look for them?

(Wait 10 seconds before repeating.)

(10 seconds)

That is the end of Part One.

Part two, part two.

You will hear some conversations. You will hear each conversation twice. Choose the correct answers for each conversation. *(10 seconds)*

Conversation 1

W: I'm so sorry I'm late Pete. It's been a nightmare of a journey.

M: That's OK, I expected the flight to be delayed because of the bad weather.

W: We weren't late; in fact the tail wind meant that we landed a few minutes early.

M: Don't tell me your luggage got lost.

W: No and before you say it, I only left my bag on the plane once you know. You'll never let me forget that, will you? I have to confess, I did something just as silly though.

M: Why, what happened?

W: Well, I got to passport control and to my horror, I realised that my passport wasn't in my bag. I was in a complete panic. I searched everywhere for it but couldn't find it.

M: So what happened?

W: Well, I couldn't get through passport control and a security guard put me in an office. I sat there for half an hour feeling very unhappy. Eventually the security guard came back with my passport in his hand, I'd left it on the plane.

M: Wow, you were lucky they found it. Let's get you home now, you must be exhausted.

W: I'm fine. I'm just glad the nightmare's over. Let's go for a drink in town.

(Wait 10 seconds before repeating.) (10 seconds)

Now, look at the questions for Conversation Two. (10 seconds)

Conversation 2

M: So, have you thought about where we might go?

W: I haven't had much chance. This Sanderson project has been taking up so much of my time lately.

M: Aren't you meant to hand in your proposal by tomorrow at the latest?

W: Yes, that's why I'm so stressed about it.

M: I wouldn't want to be in your shoes. Listen, I thought maybe a trip to the coast might be fun. It would make a change from going in to the city centre.

W: That does sound nice. We aren't taking husbands and wives with us though, are we? I could do with an evening away from the family to be honest and then Jim can look after the kids and I won't have to get a babysitter.

M: Good idea. I'll arrange everything and tell Paul and Sue in accounts too.

W: OK, I'd better get back to my work. Do you fancy lunch in that new cafe over the road later?

M: That sounds good.

(Wait 10 seconds before repeating.) (10 seconds)
Now, look at the questions for Conversation Three. (10 seconds)

Conversation 3

W: How did it go today, John?

M: Oh, it was terrible. I didn't know where to find anything and I actually got lost twice as it's such a big place.

W: Well, you are used to working in a small office. I told you you'd miss that.

M: I know but I felt so confident after doing well in the interview and the boss seems to be a good man but I think he is going to expect far too much of me. I wish I understood how their system works.

W: You know what I think about you leaving a job that you were so good at, but you've changed direction now and you'll have to learn to live with it. You should talk to your new boss. I'm sure that he'll understand that you need help to settle in.

M: Maybe I shouldn't have left City Architects after all. Still there's no point thinking that now. I'll just have to do my best to settle in as fast as possible.

W: I know, let's go out for a meal tonight. It might cheer you up and help you to relax.

M: Good idea. I can afford to treat us on my new higher salary.

(Wait 10 seconds before repeating.) (10 seconds)
That is the end of Part Two.

Part three, part three.

You will hear someone talking. You will hear the person twice. Complete the information. Write short answers of one to five words. *(1 minute)*

[beep]

Welcome to Whitehill Shopping Centre. This is a customer announcement. The shopping complex and parking facilities open at 7am and close at 9pm. Our hours of business are from 9am to 6pm; that's when you will find most shops open, although individual opening times may vary. Every Thursday, the shops in Whitehill Centre are open until 9pm for late night shopping.

There are a number of special offers available for customers today. Walkers shoe shop, on level two, has 30% off ladies' and men's shoes and 25% off all sports shoes. There are also many children's shoes at half price. Classy Clothes, on level three, have their new spring collection in this week, so you can check out what's new. All clothing from their winter collection is now 50% off. Blue Note Music, on the basement level, is offering three for two on all CDs; that's the equivalent of a third off the price! This offer is for today only so don't miss it! Finally, the Home Shop, also on the basement level, has a buy-one-get-one-free offer on all of last season's merchandise.

Whitehill Centre is also holding several events for your family's entertainment! You can take your children for free face painting at 3 o'clock outside the Cactus Cafe. This is followed at 5pm by a dance performance by pupils from St John's School. You can get a free ice-cream after the performance.

And don't forget the many options available if you feel hungry! The Cactus Cafe now specialises in pizza and pasta, in addition to sweets and coffee. And of course, their student discounts still apply. Also, the entire fourth level is a food court with food from all over the world - from Mexican, Thai, to a traditional-style cafeteria. And don't forget George's Ice-Cream Parlour, with 48 flavours of gourmet ice cream!

Finally, we want to remind customers to always keep a close eye on their personal belongings while shopping. We would like to bring to your attention that smoking is strictly prohibited in all areas of the shopping centre and all cars must be parked in the allocated parking areas. We hope you enjoy your time shopping at Whitehill Centre. Thank you.

No.3 Audio Scripts

(Wait 10 seconds before repeating.) (10 seconds)
You will now have two minutes to read through and check your answers. *(2 minutes)*
[beep]
That is the end of Part Three.

Part four, part four.
You will hear a conversation. You will hear the conversation twice. Choose the correct answers. *(20 seconds.)*

M: It was a childhood dream for Emma Milne to set up a business selling cakes just like her mother used to make. But short of money, cooking space and business-planning skills, Emma has survived emotional and financial set-backs to have the life she's always wanted.
Emma, what's it like running your own business?
W: Our weekly ingredients arrived this morning: 2000 eggs, two tonnes of nuts and bucketloads of sugar. Even today, when I see it all laid out I still get a buzz. If someone had told me ten years ago I'd make a living, let alone a successful one, out of baking, I'd never have believed it. Now I'm doing it for real. I wasn't the ideal candidate for running my own business; at college I was a dreamer; my head was always in books or over a stove inspecting a new recipe. You wouldn't have put your money on me being the girl most likely to own her own business.
M: Was that because you didn't want the commitment of having your own business?
W: It wasn't that I lacked ambition. I just didn't have the confidence or knowledge to do anything about it. I had a degree in English and once had a part-time job glazing croissants in a patisserie - hardly preparation for starting a baking business. But, as anyone who's ever had a pipe dream will tell you, there comes a point when the dream becomes a distraction. By the time I'd hit 25, I was spending hours a day wondering what it would be like to own a cake business. When that happens you have two choices. Either forget about it and spend your energy doing something else or do something about it. Sink or swim, I thought, at least I'll never say, 'What if...'
M: So what made you take the plunge?
W: Seeing my friends with good jobs and nice houses. At the time I was living with

five others in a shared house with a few temping and teaching jobs behind me. I felt inadequate. I knew I was a talented cook and had to tap into my skills if I wanted to feel better about myself.

M: And what was the inspiration for your business?

W: It came from my childhood. Baking was a big part of my family's life. I'll never forget the days Gran would come and help make little sponge cakes for my brothers and me. Every time I helped I felt that I'd achieved something, even if it only meant I'd broken an egg into a bowl.

M: What did you do to prepare for your new venture?

W: When I started out I didn't have a business plan - I just wrote all my strengths and weaknesses on a scrap of paper. Next to strengths I scrawled: talent, drive and great products. Next to weaknesses was: NO MONEY. Right from the beginning I was always honest about what I could and couldn't do - you have to be if you are doing it alone.

(Wait 10 seconds before repeating.)(10 seconds)

That is the end of Part Four.

You now have two hours and ten minutes to complete the rest of the paper.

No.3 Audio Scripts

Test 5

Part one, part one.
You will hear some short conversations. You will hear each conversation twice. Choose the correct answer for each conversation. *(15 seconds.)*

Number one. Number one. *(6 seconds)*

M: Hello, Dr. Nolin. I'm Tim Brown. I'm a student here.

W: I'm pleased to meet you, Tim.

M: Your talk was very interesting.

(Wait 10 seconds before repeating.)

(10 seconds)

Number two. Number two. *(6 seconds)*

W: Excuse me, can you tell me where to find Western Bank?

M: Certainly, it's on Bond Street, just past the park.

W: Is that far from here?

(Wait 10 seconds before repeating.)

(10 seconds)

Number three. Number three. *(6 seconds)*

M: Why did you eat the last of my cake?

W: Why do you presume it was me?

M: It was obviously you; who else could it have been?

(Wait 10 seconds before repeating.)

(10 seconds)

Number four. Number four. *(6 seconds)*

W: What adorable earrings! Do you like them?

M: Yes, they're nice.

W: Do you think the red or the blue is better?

(Wait 10 seconds before repeating.)

(10 seconds)

Number five. Number five. *(6 seconds)*

M: There might not be any coral reefs left soon.

W: Goodness! Really? Why's that?

M: It has to do with global warming. Didn't you know?

(Wait 10 seconds before repeating.)

(10 seconds)

Number six. Number six. *(6 seconds)*

W: If anyone sees you, you are going to get a fine.

M: Why?

W: You aren't allowed to smoke in here.

(Wait 10 seconds before repeating.)

(10 seconds)

Number seven. Number seven. *(6 seconds)*

M: Here; would you like one?

W: Mmm, these biscuits are delicious.

M: Please, help yourself to another.

(Wait 10 seconds before repeating.)

(10 seconds)

That is the end of Part One.

Part two, part two.

You will hear some conversations. You will hear each conversation twice. Choose the correct answers for each conversation. *(10 seconds)*

Conversation 1

W: I don't want anything too complicated. I just want to stay in touch with my son in

Australia.

M: Do you think you would prefer a laptop?

W: I don't know. What's the advantage of having a laptop?

M: Well, basically, you can take it with you wherever you go.

W: But I don't want to take it anywhere.

M: Right, a desktop will probably be what you want then. This is one of our latest models. Look, it's got a lovely flat screen.

W: But that won't fit in my cupboard.

M: Sorry Madam, I'm a bit confused.

W: Well, I'll only use it a couple of times a week so I don't want it to be cluttering up the table the rest of the time.

M: Oh, I see. Well in that case you do want a laptop because you can keep that in a cupboard or even in a drawer.

W: Lovely. Now I don't want anything too expensive.

M: I've got just the thing for you. This is a new model but it's very reasonably priced and should have everything you need.

W: Alright, lovely.

(Wait 10 seconds before repeating.) (10 seconds)
Now, look at the questions for Conversation Two. (10 seconds)

Conversation 2

M: I don't know why he got the promotion. I think you'd be far more suitable for the job.

W: I must admit, I'm very disappointed. I've worked really hard this year and I've reached all my targets.

M: Well I only met your boss once but I didn't like him.

W: Oh, he's fine really. That's why I'm so surprised because I thought he would be pleased with what I've achieved for the company.

M: We were counting on that promotion to pay for that luxury cruise. I guess it will be the usual beach holiday again then.

W: Yes, and no new car for me either. Oh well, I'm fairly happy there on the whole, so I guess there will be other chances in the future, if I work hard.

M: Yes, you're right. I'm sure you'll be the next person he'll promote. You'll just have to be patient.

(Wait 10 seconds before repeating.) (10 seconds)
Now, look at the questions for Conversation Three. (10 seconds)

Conversation 3

M: Hello Janet, I need you to do me a favour. I'm running late from the meeting with the lawyer about the Parson's project. I've only just left and I'm meant to be at the dentist's in 15 minutes.

W: Oh dear, you're not going to be there on time, are you?

M: No, and the traffic is terrible. I'm pretty close but I'm stuck in a taxi and I'll be at least 20 minutes if I'm lucky.

W: So you need me to let the dentist know that you'll be a bit late, don't you?

M: Yes, do you mind? The number is in the phonebook on my desk.

W: Don't worry, I'll phone them immediately.

M: Thanks so much, I'll be back in the office by two. See you then.

(Wait 10 seconds before repeating.) (10 seconds)
That is the end of Part Two.

Part three, part three.

You will hear someone talking. You will hear the person twice. Complete the information. Write short answers of one to five words. *(1 minute.)*

[beep]

Thank you for phoning Cinema World. For almost 30 years we've been the city's top independent cinema, celebrating world cinema in all its brilliance and diversity. Remember to visit our Cafe/Bar where you can choose from a large selection of drinks and fresh and affordable food either before or after your film.

We would also like to remind you that members of our Loyalty Club enjoy a variety of benefits, including a £1.50 discount on every ticket, 5% discount in the Cafe/Bar, an invitation to special Members' events and more. Or you can sign up for our weekly e-newsletter with film information, show times, competitions and special offers that comes straight to the inbox of your computer, so you won't miss a thing!

We now have six screens at our entertainment complex. Ticket prices are as follows. For all evening showings: under 16s - £4, adults - £6. Matinee tickets: under 16s - £3, adults - £5. There is a 10% discount for all group bookings of 6 people or more.

Matinee showings start at 2:30pm. Evening showings are at 6pm and 8pm. Tickets can be reserved by phone. Reservations can be made between 2pm and 10pm every day, but must be made at least 3 hours before the screening. This week we're showing the premier of the new romantic comedy called 'Computer Love' which stars Ben Crossly as a computer technician who falls in love over the internet. We are also showing the terrifying 'Death in the Woods 2'; the sequel to the successful 'Death in the Woods 1' which was a hit film last winter. This has an 18 certificate so it is not suitable for families or young children.

We would also like to announce our 'New Wave' Festival, showing through to the 6th of August. The British New Wave is the name given to a handful of influential films, sometimes referred to as 'kitchen sink dramas', made between 1959 and 1963. Seen by critics of the time as a step forward for British Cinema; these films heralded a move towards a more mature, intelligent portrayal of contemporary British life, and bridged the gap between the conventional studio fare of the early fifties and the hugely successful films of the 'Swinging Sixties' that were to follow.

See any three or more films in this festival and get 15% off. See any six or more films and get 25% off. See all nine films and get 35% off. These packages are available online, in person and on the phone, on both full price and concession price (tickets). Tickets must all be bought at the same time.

All programmes are advertised in the Express Newspaper and online at our website -

www.cinemaworld.com.

(Wait 10 seconds before repeating.) (10 seconds)

You will now have two minutes to read through and check your answers. *(2 minutes)*

[beep]

That is the end of Part Three.

Part four, part four.

You will hear a conversation. You will hear the conversation twice. Choose the correct answers. *(20 seconds.)*

M: Margaret Mann, the 63 year old, lives in the south of England. She has four grown-up children and has recently retired as deputy head teacher of Hollywater Special School, in Hampshire. Margaret is the winner of the Ted Wragg Award for Lifetime Achievement. Margaret, congratulations on your award. Did you always have an ambition to be a teacher?

W: Although I love teaching, I must admit that I didn't work very hard at school myself and left at 16 with no qualifications. I did various jobs afterwards but, when I found myself divorced with four young children in my early 30s, I decided it was time to do something more with my life and I studied for a degree in education with the Open University.

M: That must have been quite a challenge.

W: Although it was tough studying, working and looking after the children, it was the making of me. In the evenings I worked at Treloar School, a school for young people with physical disabilities near where I lived. I absolutely loved seeing the children develop and I got so much out of it. I still didn't know what I wanted to do after my degree. Then one day somebody said to me, "Have you ever thought about teaching children with special needs?" It was as if a light had been switched on. I had done special education as part of my degree anyway, so it seemed a natural progression.

M: Tell us about your first teaching post after graduation.

W: The first job I got was in a school for children with moderate learning difficulties. At that time the main emphasis in special needs schools was just to make sure that the children were well cared for, but I thought that they deserved a proper education, too. I wanted them to be able to fulfill their true potential. The school's motto was "What I can do, I will be", and that's the line I've taken throughout my career. We brought in the national curriculum assessment, which very few special schools did at that time. In the past, children with learning difficulties had been encouraged to concentrate on design and technology, but we became very hot on science. Many of our children reached the average science grades for their age, which was almost unheard of.

(Wait 10 seconds before repeating.) (10 seconds)
That is the end of Part Four.
You now have two hours and ten minutes to complete the rest of the paper.

About LanguageCert English Spoken Other Language（ESOL）Test

LanguageCert 考试

分为 LanguageCert ESOL Online、LanguageCert ESOL 以及 LanguageCert ESOL SELT 三种类型。

LanguageCert ESOL Online

可以通过官网 languagecert.org 或者使用微信扫描以下小程序码进行考试报名。

LanguageCert ESOL

需要通过线下授权考试中心进行报名。如果您需要了解当地考试中心的联系方式，可以使用微信扫描小程序码，随后联系在线客服获取距您最近的考试中心的联系方式。

LanguageCert ESOL SELT

SELT 考试需要在 languagecert.org 进行考试预约以及报名。如果想要进一步地了解情况，请您联系小程序的在线客服。

Answer Key

Test 1

Listening Part 1:

1.b 2.a 3.b 4.b 5.b 6.a 7.c

Listening Part 2:

1.c 2.c 3.c 4.c 5.c 6.a

Listening Part 3:

1. football tournament
2. swimming and boating
3. two counselors present
4. on the lakeshore
5. dietary needs
6. arts and crafts
7. an outdoor film

Listening Part 4:

1.a 2.b 3.c 4.c 5.b 6.c

Reading Part 1:

1.c 2.a 3.c 4.c 5.b 6.b

Reading Part 2:

1.D 2.B 3.A 4.F 5.C 6.E

Reading Part 3:

1.C 2.B 3.A 4.D 5.C 6.B 7.A

Reading Part 4:

1. November is summer
2. (they) collect fish
3. (they) go/swim south
4. (in) October
5. under their skin
6. warmer water
7. (up to) thirty (years old)

Test 2

Listening Part 1:

1.b 2.a 3.a 4.c 5.b 6.a 7.c

Listening Part 2:

1.c 2.c 3.a 4.a 5.a 6.a

Listening Part 3:

1. into three groups
2. defence
3. giving away possession
4. your game
5. around the corner
6. at 1:30 (promptly)
7. video training/an optional film

LanguageCert Communicator CEFR Level B2 ESOL/SELT 朗思全真模拟题 1

Listening Part 4:

1.a 2.b 3.c 4.a 5.c 6.b

Reading Part 1:

1.a 2.c 3.c 4.b 5.a 6.c

Reading Part 2:

1.B 2.G 3.F 4.E 5.D 6.C

Reading Part 3:

1.A 2.C 3.B 4.D 5.C 6.B 7.A

Reading Part 4:

1. take syrups/swallow pills
2. to clean (their) airways
3. soothes the throat
4. two of these: honey, blueberries, spinach, dark chocolate
5. they rise
6. more than 300
7. New Zealand

Test 3

Listening Part 1:

1.b 2.a 3.b 4.a 5.a 6.a 7.c

Listening Part 2:

1.a 2.c 3.a 4.c 5.a 6.c

Listening Part 3:

1. athletics event
2. (at) 8 am/8:00
3. (about) 20 minutes
4. all the events
5. 3/three
6. (the) refreshment tables
7. the main field

Listening Part 4:

1.a 2.b 3.a 4.b 5.c 6.a

Reading Part 1:

1.b 2.b 3.c 4.c 5.b 6.a

Reading Part 2:

1.B 2.D 3.F 4.C 5.A 6.E

Reading Part 3:

1.C 2.A 3.B 4.D 5.C 6.A 7.D

Reading Part 4:

1. a (colourful) puzzle
2. solving real problems
3. a long time
4. it compares solutions
5. a few weeks
6. scheduling airplane flights
7. jump over it

Test 4

Listening Part 1:

1.c 2.b 3.a 4.c 5.b 6.b 7.c

Listening Part 2:

1.c 2.b 3.c 4.b 5.c 6.a

Listening Part 3:

1. Thursday
2. half price
3. 24 hours/today (only)
4. dance performance
5. hungry
6. Cactus Cafe
7. strictly prohibited

Listening Part 4:

1.a 2.c 3.a 4.b 5.c 6.a

Reading Part 1:

1.a 2.a 3.a 4.a 5.c 6.b

Reading Part 2:

1.C 2.E 3.F 4.A 5.G 6.D

Reading Part 3:

1.B 2.D 3.C 4.D 5.B 6.A 7.C

Reading Part 4:

1. compensate financially or arrange financial compensation
2. the Crown Court
3. make decisions alone
4. police officers/ keep the law
5. the jury
6. small claims
7. the Coroner's Court

Test 5

Listening Part 1:

1.b 2.c 3.c 4.a 5.c 6.a 7.a

Listening Part 2:

1.b 2.c 3.c 4.c 5.a 6.c

Listening Part 3:

1. Loyalty Club members
2. computer (inbox)
3. 10pm / 22:00
4. families or young children
5. August 6th
6. the same time
7. the (cinema's) website: (www.cinemaworld.com)

Listening Part 4:

1.c 2.b 3.a 4.c 5.c 6.a

LanguageCert Communicator CEFR Level B2 ESOL/SELT 朗思全真模拟题 1

Reading Part 1:

1.c   2.c   3.a   4.b   5.a   6.b

Reading Part 2:

1.B   2.G   3.D   4.E   5.A   6.F

Reading Part 3:

1.C   2.A   3.D   4.A   5.D   6.B   7.C

Reading Part 4:

1. Lack of willpower

2. Marks and Spencer

3. (their) waistline(s)/tummies/tummy

4. obesity in children

5. nine years

6. time consuming (and very costly)

7. a reward/mini-rewards